THE
INTERACTIVE
MANAGER

THE
INTERACTIVE
MANAGER

A SELF ASSESSMENT AND DEVELOPMENT PROGRAMME

Sukhwant Bal

Software Developer: Mark Statham

This book is dedicated to my wife Kully, my daughters Amarat and Simran and my mother and father

First published in 1995

Kogan Page Limited
120 Pentonville Road
London N1 9JN

© Sukhwant Bal, 1995

British Library Cataloguing in Publication Data

A CIP record for this book is available from the British Library.

ISBN 0 7494 1708 0

Typeset by Saxon Graphics Ltd, Derby
Printed and bound in Great Britain by Clays Ltd, St Ives plc

CONTENTS

ACKNOWLEDGEMENTS

In developing the book and software, I owe my gratitude to so many people. First, my sincere thanks to Mark Statham for his dedication and unflinching conviction in programming and developing the software. Had it not been for Mark I would not have been able to complete this book. To a friend and an unsung hero, thank you. I know he would want me to thank his wife Ann for her support over the many months he worked on the software.

I would like to thank my colleagues at Kiddy and Partners and Creating Insights Press for allowing me time to complete this project. My special thanks to Chris Kiddy, Brian Baxter and Tony Clarry. Special thanks also go to Amanda Potts for her hard work in getting the diagrams desk-top published. Her preparedness to help and get involved with the project has been a breath of fresh air. For checking the software and providing suggestions for improvement, my appreciation goes to Tom Sopwith. I would also like to thank my former colleagues at PA Consulting Group, who taught me so much and are too numerous to mention here.

I would also like to thank the many clients I have worked with over the past six years; again, too numerous to mention. Without the experience they provided, many of the case histories could not have been written. On which subject, special thanks to Lorren Wyatt, Director of Human Resources at Birmingham Midshires Building Society.

My appreciation also goes to the Kogan Page team, who were prepared to run with a project which had not been tested before. I hope it proves to be successful for all concerned. My special thanks to Dolores Black for her support and guidance.

Finally, thanks to my wife (and best friend) who was prepared to put up with a husband tucked away in his study most evenings and weekends, forsaking all the chores and responsibilities around the house. Without her support, humour and friendship this project would not have been accomplished.

FOREWORD

The old deal has gone for ever. Organizations will never again offer training and development for the next rung up the ladder. The rung has been knocked out in the recent delayering, and they can't afford it anyway. The new manager or professional has to be, in Robert Waterman's term, career resilient. He or she has to be capable of developing themself, either with or, more usually, without their organization's support.

This learning package is designed with the career-resilient individual in mind. It recognizes the old prescription of learning from experience cannot suffice in the present rate of change. It's just too slow. Reflection on our experience is necessary, but it's no longer sufficient. Rather, we need to anticipate the changes that are already on the horizon and prepare for them.

Sukhwant Bal has helped crack this difficult but necessary task. He has picked out both the eternal verities and the new competencies. The skills we will always need include decision making, communication and motivation, but this package goes well beyond these. It focuses on managing change, team work, coaching, and leadership – just those areas which the flexible firm of the future requires.

When you have completed this package, you will certainly have developed further in some of these important areas. More vitally for your own career success, you will have acquired some more general skills: understanding how to assess yourself and how you can learn better are two examples. In particular, you will have become able to formulate realistic and yet personally profitable development plans.

How does our author deliver these desirable outcomes? This package uses its component parts to optimum advantage. The software helps us with the self-analysis and gives us the immediate feedback needed to ensure this sort of learning. The text combines theory and practice to enable us to reflect upon our experience and broaden our horizons.

The managers of the future will depend for their survival on their employability. Instead of going for a better remuneration deal, they will change jobs in the hope of further development and hence further employability. This package will add to your employability quotient – the true differentiator in the labour market of the twenty-first century.

So what will this brave new world look like to the career-resilient manager? Essentially it wll be a forum for negotiations – for doing deals. To get good deals you need to know a few things about negotiating. In particular, you need to know what you have to offer. When you have completed this package, you'll know what you've got to offer. What's more, you'll have more to offer than you thought you had. The core employees of the lean organization of the future will certainly want the competencies developed in the package. They will also want the ability to learn – and learning how better to learn may be the most important benefit you will receive.

Peter Herriot
Director of Research
Sundridge Park Management Centre

INTRODUCTION TO THE INTERACTIVE PACKAGE

How often have you had the opportunity of receiving informative feedback on your strengths and development needs? How often have you wondered where your real strengths lie? How often have you considered what attributes would be essential to progress in your management career?

If your answer to any of these questions is 'not often' then *The Interactive Manager* book and integrated software will give you a unique opportunity to assess your own strengths and weaknesses in your own time, at your own pace, in complete privacy.

Book and software have been designed as a complementary package that allows you to update your self-assessment and gauge your progress.

This package is about enabling you to do things for yourself through *self-insight*. The package is designed to enable you to learn more about your management style, your strengths and development needs and to apply key messages from the package to your own situation. Think of it as a personal guide. The more you ask of it, the more you get in return. The package is intended for anyone who wishes to:

- improve their managerial skills
- learn more about themselves
- acquire new insights into the world of work
- prepare themselves for the future
- learn to learn for themselves.

Self-insight is an important feature of the above headings. Indeed, self-insight and self-development are the key themes here.

It is now the view of a growing number of line and personnel managers that self-development will be critical in the business environment of the future. Self-renewal and the learning organization have been regularly cited in management journals, the key message being that to excel in a highly competitive environment, organizations need to adapt and learn quickly from events. But explore this in further detail and the real message is that individuals – the people at the sharp end – need to continually update their knowledge and skill base. Through self-insight they need to evaluate their own effectiveness and take the necessary steps to improve their own performance.

This book is about helping you to start this journey on gaining a better understanding of your own strengths and development needs.

TAKING CONTROL IN A CHANGING WORLD

Change is a business constant. In every sector, competition is extremely intensive; only the fittest will survive. Responsiveness and adaptation are critical at an organizational and individual level if businesses are to thrive. Organizations can re-engineer themselves to produce flatter organizational structures, reduce their work-force, employ less complicated internal mechanisms and use systems which enable them to get closer to the customer. But what can individuals do?

There are three fundamental mind-shifts required from individuals if they are to be effective in the corporate environment of the future:

- Mind-shift 1: Keep what works and throw out what does not
- Mind-shift 2: Strive to keep transforming yourself
- Mind-shift 3: Accept that stability and job security are things of the past.

KEEP WHAT WORKS AND THROW OUT WHAT DOES NOT

Responsiveness and adaptability can only come about if an individual is prepared to try working practices which are innovative and perhaps unconventional. Being adaptable means placing less reliance on past behaviour and experience and more on actual results in the here-and-now. There needs to be a constant evaluation of how effective different strategies are: if they are not producing positive outcomes they need to be dumped.

This *mind-set*, however, is unlikely to come easily: after all, we base so much of our behaviour on past experience. The past actually provides us with a sense of identity and of assurance. 'Because we have done it before we can do it again.' The irony, however, is that what we have learnt in the past can be a barrier to our effectiveness in the future. There needs to be a continual evaluation of the skills and knowledge one has with the requirements of the present. The message is that if what you are currently doing is not producing desired outcomes, then try something different. You need to be ready to let go of skills or behaviour which are not producing beneficial results and adopt new skills and behaviours – a process which does not come readily unless you are 'geared-up'. This leads on to the second mind-shift.

STRIVE TO KEEP TRANSFORMING YOURSELF

The mind-shift here is that self-development is a continuous process. It is not so much the transformation which is difficult, but the awareness which lies behind it. In other words, how do you know that it is time to acquire new skills or information? Does someone tap you on the shoulder and tell you it's time? Actually, that's not too far from the truth. Many organizations are creating 'bottom-up leadership' cultures, where individuals have responsibility to provide colleagues and team members with constructive feedback on performance.

One way this can be achieved at a formal level is through *'all-round'* performance appraisal systems which elicit feedback from bosses, colleagues and subordinates. These comments are 'aggregated' and provide indicators of how others view your strengths and development needs. Other organizations are linking customers' feedback to pay and performance ratings – again, in a bid to get individuals to acquire new skills and behaviours. The acquisition and application of new skills are likely to be highly attractive to any prospective employer. This leads on to the third point.

ACCEPT THAT STABILITY AND JOB SECURITY ARE THINGS OF THE PAST

The third mind-shift is the realization that business empires come and go in ever-decreasing time scales. To equip themselves for this changing world of work, managers need to acquire both 'hard' and 'soft' skills. The hard skills are technical and managerial expertise – the ability to deliver business objectives. The soft skills are to do with the less tangible factors: self-insight, self-awareness and adaptability. The key to a manager's marketability in the future will be the extent to which he or she has both hard and soft skills. The soft skills enable managers to adapt to different business environments and be able to transfer their skills from one industry to another. As new industries emerge and others near extinction, the executives of the future will need to adopt new game-plans and strategies. It will be their ability to learn, acquire new skills and information and abandon the skills they do not need which will enable them to thrive.

STRUCTURE OF THE BOOK

This book is designed so that chapters follow the same format and can be read independently. Each chapter includes the following sections:

- Over to you
- The business case
- Putting it into practice
- Key principles
- Key action and learning points
- Case histories and personal views
- Summary.

The book's primary aim is to encourage you to gain greater self-awareness and insight into issues. It is for this reason that the 'open-ended' sections have been included: 'over to you' and key action and learning points. The software, too, is designed to be flexible: it is up to you to discover your own strengths and development needs and what this means for you.

The 12 chapters

Over the past five years I have worked with numerous organizations, helping them to identify managerial behaviours critical for effectiveness. It soon became apparent that there were a number of attributes which seemed to occur on a regular basis, irrespective of the culture and sector of the organization. The diagram below encapsulates the main (but not all) attributes considered important for managerial excellence. The Job Analysis and Self-insight Questionnaires in the software are designed around this model. Chapters 5, 9, 11 and 12 have further supporting questionnaires.

A PROFILE OF MANAGERIAL EXCELLENCE

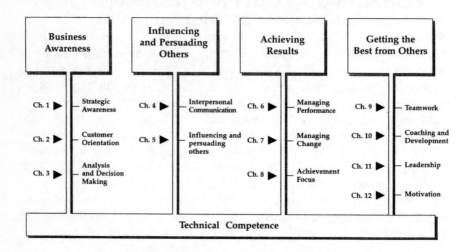

OVERVIEW OF THE QUESTIONNAIRES
INCLUDED IN THE SOFTWARE

- **Job Analysis Questionnaire:** this encourages you to think about your role and the behaviours you consider to be critical for effective performance. Likely to take 30 to 40 minutes to complete.

- **Self-insight Questionnaire:** this is designed to get you to think about your own strengths and development needs. The software will then provide you with a comparison of the Job Analysis and Self-insight Questionnaires. Likely to take 30 to 40 minutes to complete.

- **Preferred Leadership Style**: this will provide you with information on your main leadership styles. Likely to take 10 to 15 minutes to complete.

- **Influencing Style Questionnaire:** this is designed to provide you with information on how you are most likely to influence and persuade others. Likely to take 10 to 15 minutes to complete.

- **Team Style Questionnaire:** this questionnaire encourages you to think about what roles you are most likely to be suited to in a team situation, based on your personality. Likely to take 10 to 15 minutes to complete.

- **Motivation Index:** the extent to which you are motivated in your current role and the extent to which you in turn motivate others is the purpose of this particular questionnaire. Likely to take 15 to 20 minutes to complete both sections.

GETTING THE MOST FROM THE BOOK AND SOFTWARE

Here are some suggestions on how you might get the most from this package.

Review

This is designed to help you focus on your career to date, establish what the main landmarks have been, and to help you gain some perspective on what you would like to get from this book. The review section is included at the end of this introduction. It would be useful for you to complete it before you actually start reading the book and using the software.

Clarify

Complete the Job Analysis Questionnaire to gain an appreciation of the main attributes you consider important for your current role. Then go on to complete the Self-insight Questionnaire, which is designed to clarify your perceptions of your strengths and development needs against the enclosed model. The software will enable you to compare the two questionnaires and provide you with information on relative strengths and development needs. Check how these stack up against what you wrote under the Personal Review.

Investigate

Having established the areas you wish to develop further, refer to the relevant chapters in the book and make use of the open-ended sections designed for your input. Writing down some of the issues you are facing at work often helps clarify the nature of the problem. In addition, you will be able to monitor your own progress at a later stage. Some of the other questionnaires in the software may be of further use to you.

Actions

Through the relevant case histories, key principles and learning points, decide what actions you need to take to address your development needs. Be as creative as you can, perhaps teaming up with other colleagues to see how you

GETTING THE MOST FROM THE BOOK AND SOFTWARE

**Step 1
REVIEW**

Complete the personal **review** section. This is designed to help clarify:-

- what you hope to get from the book
- how you see your strengths
- how you see your development needs
- some career directions

**Step 2
CLARIFY**

Use the software to help **clarify** and focus your thoughts on your strengths and development needs, against twelve core managerial competencies

**Step 3
INVESTIGATE**

Through the software, identify the areas you would like to focus on further, and through the chapters, **investigate**:-

- how and why they are important in business
- how they apply in practice
- the theory behind them, and...
- case histories relating to them

**Step 4
ACTIONS**

Decide on what **actions** you propose to take, to address:-

- specific issues you are facing in the work context
- issues specific to you

**Step 5
MONITOR**

Monitor the progress you make. Keep referring to the individual chapters to keep track of key points

can support each other and provide constructive feedback. The 'Over to you' section in the software, too, has further information on this.

Monitor

It is important you monitor the progress you make. To that end, complete the Self-insight Questionnaire a second time and compare how your responses have changed. Re-read chapters and evaluate whether you have implemented and adopted some of the key messages in them. Keep track of progress using the 'Over to you' section in the software.

PERSONAL REVIEW SECTION

Career History

1. What have been the main stages of your career?

2 How have your motivations and aspirations changed over time?

3. What have been your main achievements and successes?

4. What single achievement has given you most career satisfaction?

Present Role

1. What elements of your current role give you the greatest satisfaction?

2. Which elements of your role do you like least?

3. How do you think your boss would describe your main strengths and development needs?

4. Which of your strengths and skills do you feel the organization is not making best use of?

The Future

1. What are your aspirations?

2. What are the gaps between the skills and experience you have now and those you'll need to achieve your goals?

3. What key learning points from the past would you want to take into the future?

4. What do you need to start doing today to ensure you fulfil your aspirations?

Section 1

BUSINESS AWARENESS

Chapter 1

STRATEGIC AWARENESS

Strategy is the art of creating value.
(Normann and Ramirez, 1993)

WHAT YOU CAN EXPECT

After reading this chapter, you will have a better understanding of:

- the key features of corporate strategy

- how you can improve your level of strategic awareness

- the essentials of strategic management

- how value can be created through strategic awareness

- how strategy and differentiation are linked

- the role of strategy in determining the values and culture of an organization

- why strategy needs to be a continuously evolving process

———— OVER TO YOU ————

1. How much involvement do you have in wider strategic issues and what type of involvement has it been?

2. What are the main things you want to learn from this chapter and how might they be applied to your current circumstances?

3. How do you currently add value for your internal and external customers?

4. What information does the software reveal on: (a) the importance of strategic awareness for your role and (b) your strengths and development needs?

THE BUSINESS CASE

Corporate strategy forms the cornerstone of any business: it is the 'blue-print' which determines what products and services will be offered and how these will be delivered to generate a healthy return for shareholders. Strategic awareness is more than articulating a vision and mission statement, it is about a wholesale appraisal of the market place, competitors and customers and understanding how this impacts on the business. Having a strategic awareness enables a manager to use this information meaningfully to create value by aligning the activities of the organization with the needs of customers. Those organizations which excel in aligning with the needs of their customers gain a competitive edge and continue to do so by evolving the way they create value. For these organizations, creating value for customers becomes the single most important strategic objective. Strategic awareness for managers is important in three critical areas.

Defining what the business stands for

This is perhaps the most critical element of strategic awareness: defining the values important to the organization. Values are important in clarifying what the organization represents: it might be to be the 'best in class', to provide the maximum return to shareholders, to be the most innovative company in the sector, or to provide the highest quality of service to customers. These values send out a clear message to the organization of what we are in business for and where energy and resources should be focused. Understanding strategic values enables managers, amongst other things, to make more informed decisions and manage others' performance far more meaningfully.

Creating competitive advantage

The purpose of corporate strategy is to create an organization which *delivers value* to its customers and its shareholders. This can only be achieved through creating competitive advantages – features which are difficult for competitors to imitate and which are perceived as being distinct by customers. Competitive advantage may be achieved through having greater product variety, or through having products with more features, produced to a higher specification and more cost-effectively than competitors. These advantages however, need to be 'engineered' in line with strategic objectives. At its most fundamental level, creating a competitive advantage entails linking three important questions:

- what do our customers want?
- how can we meet their needs most effectively?
- how can we differentiate ourselves from the competition?

23

Continuous improvement and innovation

Managers who demonstrate strategic awareness continuously seek to add value to products and services, in line with the changing needs of customers. Continuously creating value for customers can only be achieved by being geared to do so. Many leading organizations such as Sony and Sharp, for example, have identified what their core skills as an organization are and have built their businesses around these. In the case of Sony, it excels in the miniaturization of products – the Walkman being a case in point. Sharp uses leading-edge technology in producing high resolution liquid crystal screens. Continuously adapting and innovating the match between what an organization excels in and the needs of the market place is a highly effective and efficient way to compete.

The bottom line is that in today's competitive market place managers need to have strategic awareness for, as the opening quote suggests, it is the means by which lasting value is created for customers and shareholders.

PUTTING IT INTO PRACTICE

This section looks at the practical steps you as a manager can take to improve your own and others' awareness of strategic issues. This section is structured around these four points:

1. Strategic awareness is critical if managers are to manage a department effectively;
2. Managers need to get into the habit of identifying what leading organizations do which enables them to excel;
3. The implementation of strategy needs to be based on knowing the strengths and weaknesses of the business, the opportunities which can be exploited and the threats which must be considered;
4. Effectively implementing strategic objectives depends on a manager having systems and processes in place which provide regular feedback on performance.

1. Understanding the role of strategy in business

In order to manage a business effectively, individuals need to be strategically aware. While many managers are not actively involved in defining the strategic objectives of the business, they are involved in their implementation. This strategic awareness enables managers to understand and rationalize the business case behind change and to manage their divisions/units in line with these broader objectives. Strategic awareness is also fundamental to having a practical appreciation of critical business parameters, such as: whether customers are getting added-value, how the business as a whole is performing financially and how your own unit is contributing to the business. Some of these points are taken up in more detail in the next section.

2. Benchmarking 'best-practice'

To be effective in achieving key business parameters, it is important to know what the standards of excellence are. Benchmarking is the practice of forming a mutually beneficial arrangement with an organization which you and others have identified as having standards of excellence. By knowing what these organizations actually do and how they achieve excellence, you can begin to narrow the gap between your own standards and those of 'best-practice' organizations. Benchmarking does not have to be done with organizations in your own sector – in most situations it involves building a collaborative relationship with organizations you are not in direct competition with.

Alternatively, benchmarking can be done internally, where several divisions exist and 'best practice' can be shared. Take for example, the case of Unipart, the automotive components manufacturer. Its chief executive, John Neill, learned 'lean' manufacturing techniques from Honda and Toyota's British plants and won the UK Factory of the Year Award in 1989 and 1993. John Neill was acutely aware that unless the business could capture the lessons learnt from many of the Japanese firms it supplied it would very quickly fall behind. Neill created 'Unipart University'. He made each business responsible for finding the best practice in its field, customizing it for Unipart and then teaching it to the other businesses and their partners. Neill had identified the strategic importance of lean manufacturing techniques. The starting point was to identify best practice and then to have the internal processes in place to bring this about:

> 'Our vision, is to build the world's best lean enterprise. That means continuously integrating training, or should I say learning, into the decision-making systems of the company' (cited in Womack and Jones, 1994).

3. Contextualizing strategy with a SWOT analysis

So far then, you have a firm appreciation of the *direction* the business is going in and how this impacts your own division. You have identified what the key business drivers are which will *differentiate* you from the competition and enable the business objectives to be achieved. Furthermore, you have *benchmarked* what the 'best-in-class' is for these key business drivers. What next? It is important to contextualize strategy with a SWOT (strengths, weaknesses, opportunities, threats) analysis. This will enable your division or organization to identify the strengths it can capitalize on, as well as weaknesses which could adversely impact these key drivers. The following example might help clarify this point:

At the time of writing this section, the Securities and Investment Board (SIB) has recommended that individuals given the wrong advice on pensions are entitled to compensation. This recommendation obviously has very far reaching consequences for the life assurance industry. Let's assume that 'The Typical Life Assurance Co.' had been extremely successful selling its policies through commission-only sales people. Even though over a third of customers surrendered their policies within the first year, the business was highly profitable. More recently, it decided to look at its strategic direction in the light of great change and competition in the industry and decided that it would differentiate itself from all the other companies in the market place through the quality of its service and advice. The *opportunity* of competing through building long-term relationships with customers was the main focus of the business. However, if the company were to take a closer look at *itself* via a SWOT analysis, it would realize that:

- its *strengths* were its network of sales consultants throughout the UK, who were 'hungry' for success;
- a major *weakness* was that these independently minded, commission-only sales consultants had very little 'loyalty' towards The Typical Life Assurance Co.;
- the *threats* in the market place were predominantly to do with customer perceptions of the industry and the potential financial losses in having to compensate customers for poor advice.

Given this background, you can see the difficulty in wanting to provide better quality advice and building long-term relationships and implementing this change with independently minded, commission-only sales consultants.

In short, meeting the needs of the market place needs to be balanced with looking inwards and assessing whether the strategic objectives are realistic given the strengths and weaknesses of the organization. Appreciating what the core competencies and capabilities of your organization/division are enables you to focus on your strengths and get the maximum benefit from them. Case History 1.1 provides more detailed information on the value of core competencies and capabilities.

4. Incorporating strategic objectives into business unit objectives

At the business planning stage, most managers will have been given the overall strategic objectives of the business and will be required to apply these to their own business units. How exactly are strategic objectives implemented at the business unit level? Take, for example, the hypothetical case of a business unit manager working for Halcyon Health Authority. Key features of the Health Authority's strategic objectives are:

'we seek to excel in anticipating and responding to the needs of patients...and to provide treatment in the most efficient and effective way'.

These objectives were then defined more precisely in performance standards, before being handed to managers. In putting together their individual business plans the business unit manager's time was taken up by identifying how these performance standards would be achieved. For example, one specific performance target was:

'to improve patient satisfaction levels by 15%'

A recent survey monitoring levels of patient satisfaction revealed in the Out-Patient Department the following grievances:

- The length of time they have to wait for an appointment to see a specialist.
- The time they have to spend in the waiting area before they are seen by the specialist.
- The lack of information they have on arrival, as to how long they will be there and who the specialist is.
- The lack of information given to them by the specialist on their prognosis and what they could be doing for themselves as 'after-care'.

In improving the levels of patient satisfaction by 15 per cent, the goals in the manager's business plan were to address the above issues, by providing more of what patients wanted; by addressing the cause of many of these problems and by having systems in place which would provide regular feedback on the performance indicators. This would enable the manager to respond quickly to performance indicators which were showing that interventions were not bringing about the desired outcomes.

Chapter 6 on managing performance describes in more detail how strategic objectives can be effectively achieved at the business unit level.

THE KEY PRINCIPLES OF STRATEGIC AWARENESS

There are some basic principles which capture the essence of strategic awareness, which relate back to the three questions raised in 'Creating competitive advantage', earlier in this chapter: what do our customers want, how can we meet their needs most effectively and how can we differentiate ourselves from competitors? These three questions are addressed in this section.

Understanding your market place, your customers and how your products/services are performing

It is very rare for organizations to have a single product or service which they sell to a clearly defined market place. If this were the case strategic planning would be a relatively straightforward process. The reality is that organizations typically offer several products and services to different target groups in a variety of markets. Products themselves will have different levels of penetration in the different market places. One of the most widely used models for understanding how products/services are matched to the needs of the market place is the Boston matrix shown in Figure 1.1.

Dogs are in the weakest position, for they have a low market share in a low growth market. These products and services need to be looked at carefully: either they should be disposed of or radically changed.

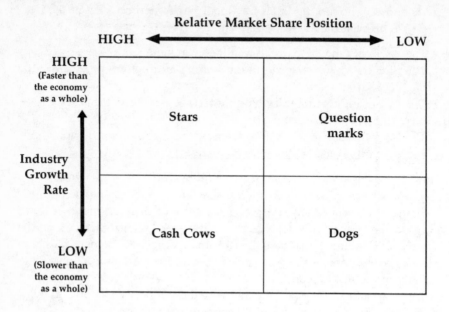

Figure 1.1 *The Boston matrix*

Cash cows are products/services which have high relative market share, in a low growth industry. Subsequently, they require little investment and generate lots of cash.

Question marks require large injections of cash to turn their fortunes around and turn them into stars.

Stars are in the ideal position. They fund their own development, having high relative market share in a high growth industry.

Where do you need to focus for the future?

Having established the positioning of your products and services, it is important to look ahead and decide where they should be positioned to meet the future needs of your target population. The positioning will determine how the organization needs to adapt and what implications this will have on the business as a whole. Looking at Figure 1.2 for example, concentrating on new markets and new products would require a far more entrepreneurial culture and strategy than focusing on existing markets with existing products/services. The strategy of moving into the entrepreneurial stage will have a lot to do with how the products/services are currently positioned, eg 'Dogs' or 'Cash cows' and the short and longer term needs of customers.

Finding ways to add value to your customers

An important feature of an organization's strategy is based on how it will compete in the market place and how it will differentiate its products/services.

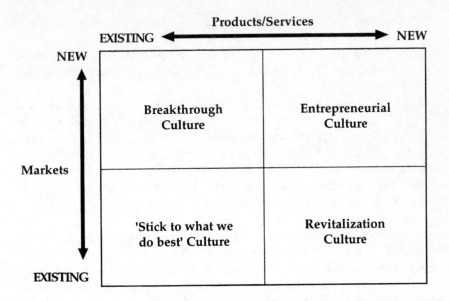

Figure 1.2 *The relationship between products, markets and culture*

The value chain model put forward by Michael Porter in his influential book – *Competitive Advantage: Creating and sustaining superior performance* – breaks down the firm into its strategically relevant activities. Porter's model shows how a firm gains competitive advantage by performing these strategically important activities more cheaply or better than its rivals. These primary activities can be divided into the following categories:

1. **Supplier relationships**: added value here could be in the form of suppliers providing better quality products, more flexibly and at times best suited to the business. Firms such as Toyota, Nissan and Honda are renowned for forming long-term partnerships with their suppliers, which, they would argue, enables them to produce better quality cars. A firm's relationship with its suppliers will often entail sharing information and 'best practice'. Toyota, for example, regularly sends project teams to work with suppliers, to identify where improvements and cost savings can be made.
2. **Operations**: is the production and manufacturing of products. In service organizations, operational issues would be around how effectively information is managed and how it is put to use. Adding value at this stage would be providing this process more efficiently and cost-effectively than the competition. For example, companies such as Volvo offer 'customized cars', where a prospective customer identifies the model, colour, engine-size and extras they want and the car is then made to those specifications, within days at no extra cost to them and savings for the business.
3. **Delivery**: this entails getting your products or services to your customers.

Adding value during this process might be offering same-day delivery or providing far more convenient ways of collecting purchases: take the case of Argos, for example, where the shopper orders from a catalogue, rather than having to walk around large department stores searching for the item they want.

4. **Marketing and sales:** is the process of encouraging people to buy and providing the means for them to do so. Added value at this stage might be the ease with which customers are able to buy your products/services. There is the example of Direct Line, where buyers can purchase home and car insurance over the phone; or McDonald's 'Drive-thrus', where customers have the convenience of buying goods without having to get out of their cars. Other companies such as The Body Shop and The Co-operative Bank focus their marketing campaigns on high-profile issues. The stance these organizations take ensures they are easily differentiated from the competition.

5. **Service:** is the provision of advice during the buying process which helps the customer make a decision. This should also extend to the after-sales service. Adding value during this process can vary dramatically, but could entail employing staff who are fully knowledgeable on products, or staff who offer impartial advice and are not on commission for one product/service, or service which is very fast and efficient.

Case History 1.1

Capabilities and Core Competencies: Their Strategic Value

An important contribution to corporate strategy has recently been provided by the concept of core competencies and capabilities. The main exponents of this work are Hamel and Prahalad on the area of core competencies and Stalk, Evans and Shulman on the area of capabilities. These authors contend that leading organizations develop corporate strategies which focus on their core competencies and capabilities. Core competencies can broadly be described as the expertise the organization has in-house; while capabilities is to do with the integration of these core competencies with external organizations, who are involved with the supply and delivery of your products/services.

Core competencies are defined by Hamel and Prahalad as the combination of individual technologies and production skills that underlie a company's various product lines. They highlight how organizations such as Sony have capitalized on their core competence of developing miniaturized technology, which they transferred and applied to a range of products, such as videocameras, notebook computers and the Sony Walkman. Other organizations such as Honda have developed core competencies in the design and manufacture of highly efficient and reliable engines. Their portfolio of products includes cars, lawnmowers and motorcycles. In the case of Canon, core competencies in optics and imaging have enabled them to enter the photocopier, laser printer and camera markets.

Stalk, Evans and Shulman contend that core competencies only partly explain why leading organizations are successful. Capabilities are also important; they are the processes which are of strategic significance to the business and which meet the needs of the customer more effectively than the competition. The authors suggest that there are four basic principles of capabilities-based competition:

1. Business processes should be the starting point in developing corporate strategy, rather than products and markets.
2. Competitive success depends on transforming a company's key processes into strategic capabilities that consistently provide superior value to the customer.
3. Strategic investment in infrastructure to support these capabilities is essential.
4. The chief executive has a critical role to play in championing and integrating capabilities across functions.

So how do capabilities work in practice? The authors describe how Honda built its reputation not just on the quality of its products, but with the relationships it built with its dealers. Honda managed its dealer network to offer quality of service and managed them so that they would become successful business people. A medical equipment company responded to the threat from competitors to under-cut them and make in-roads into their market share, by focusing on capabilities. By identifying how customers bought their products in the first place and where and how they got repeat business, this organization focused its resources on providing 'on-site reps'. These service representatives knew the needs of customers better than their competitors and were on-hand to attend to their needs. This is yet another example of how a strategic direction was set by focusing on business processes.

A Personal View 1.2

New Directions in Competitive Strategies

Here I would like to draw on current trends in the market place and how these will influence the future direction of competitive strategies. The starting point of this discussion is that traditional grounds of competitive advantage are rapidly becoming industry standards. Take the example of Japanese car manufacturers who gained market share from British manufacturers through better quality of build, providing more features for a lower or comparable price. Today, however, quality of build, price competition and added value are common features of most of the mass car producers. In a rapidly changing market place, traditional differentiators can now be copied by competitors relatively quickly. At best, technology offers a six to twelve month lead on competitors before they too will develop a similar product, often with higher specifications. Better management information systems and manufacturing processes are resulting in production costs being fairly consistent amongst home producers. So-called 'hard' factors are fairly easy to define and imitate. So what are the new and emerging trends in *sustaining competitive advantage*?

The first is a move into areas which are difficult to imitate and the second is in increasing value to customers. I have already touched on how some organizations such as Honda, Sony and Canon have focused on core competencies and capabilities as a means of differentiating themselves from competitors. The whole area of core competencies is based on commercially exploiting your technical superiority over the competition and continually developing the strength of these core competencies. For other organizations such as British Airways, McDonald's and Marks and Spencer, quality of service is a key 'soft' differentiator which is less easy to define and imitate. This type of competitive advantage is often based on the *perceptions* customers have of an organization, which have built up over time through advertising campaigns or through a long-standing reputation.

The second area of adding value is more interesting altogether. The game plan here is to compete through integrating and multiplying values. The concept used by de Bono (1993) is 'surpetition' (*sur* meaning 'above'), rather than 'competition'; in other words, leading organizations choose to compete in their *own race*, rather than run in the same race as their competitors. Take the example of British Airways: it has chosen to create and integrate new value systems. Through enormous investment in information technology, BA is able to book you a seat over the phone, giving precedence to customers with a higher currency value; customers collect Airmiles, enabling them to get discounts on future flights; and can get additional discounts and Airmiles through the special deals BA negotiates with car rental firms and major hotel chains. If you need to get to a destination BA does not directly serve, the chances are they have an alliance with a national airline which does, providing you with the convenience of not having to collect your baggage and check in again. Its collaboration with telecommunications companies means that it can offer one-number international mobile phones. Regular fliers can also get a range of other benefits. This *added-value* to customers and the *integration* of benefits – from being able to book seats over the phone to getting discounts on car rentals – is what is meant by *new competitive strategies*.

THE KEY ACTION AND LEARNING POINTS

1. What have been the main learning points for you in this chapter?

2. How will you address some of the issues you wrote in the 'Over to you' section? What are the timescales you are setting and what resources/help will you require?

3. What actions might you personally want to take to increase your strategic awareness; ie, try to get exposure to more strategically-oriented work; attend strategic awareness workshops, etc?

LEARNING POINTS FROM THE
CASE HISTORIES

Case History 1.1 introduces the value of core competencies and capabilities to corporate strategy. Core competencies are the skills and knowledge an organization has which enables it to add value to customers. Capabilities are much wider skills which allow an organization to integrate its services and products with its suppliers and dealers. By identifying its core competencies and exploring more creative and value-adding ways of getting its products and services to customers, an organization can begin to compete more intelligently.

Case History 1.2 reviews how leading organizations are developing ever more innovative ways of differentiating themselves from the competition. While focusing on core competencies and capabilities is one route to differentiation, the other is to integrate the way value is added to the customer. One such example is British Airways, which is creating its own value system in the convenience it offers customers through its strategic alliances.

SUMMARY

The business case

To manage a business effectively managers need to be strategically aware. Strategic awareness provides a framework by which managers are able to offer value to customers, through aligning customers' needs with business processes. Successful organizations encourage managers to take a wider view and to work for the good of the business, rather than their personal 'fiefdom'. An understanding of the bigger picture enables managers to continuously seek improvements, and to introduce 'best-practice' into what they do.

Putting it into practice

Strategic awareness in practice is evident by the things managers do, the insight they have of the business and the market place they compete in. This means setting standards of excellence, through having benchmarked what leading organizations do. It means getting a more thorough appreciation of the strengths of the business and how these can be maximized, while the weaknesses which hamper the successful implementation of strategic objectives are addressed. By completing a SWOT analysis of their business unit, a manager is in a much better position to identify the core competencies and capabilities which will enable strategic objectives to be achieved.

The key principles

There are a number of key principles which form the cornerstone of strategic awareness. These principles are based on three core issues:

What market place are we in and who are our customers?
How competitive are our products/services and are they meeting the needs of our customers?
How can we add value to what we offer and enable us to differentiate ourselves from the competition?

The use of the Boston matrix provides some information on elements of the first two questions. Figure 1.2 also provides a useful framework for thinking about how entering a different market place will impact the values and culture of the organization.

Chapter 2

CUSTOMER ORIENTATION

It's quite amazing the number of businesses which fail to take even the simplest of steps. What does our customer want from us? Why not ask?
(O'Driscoll, 1993)

WHAT YOU CAN EXPECT

After reading this chapter, you will have a better understanding of:

■ how leading organizations excel in customer service

■ the different ways customer service can be implemented

■ the benefits which result from being customer-oriented

■ the practical steps which form the basis of effective customer service

■ how customer service applies to the public sector

■ the organizational factors which influence customer service

■ how key business processes are driven by the need to be customer-oriented

OVER TO YOU

1. How customer-oriented is your organization/department?

2. Who are your customers and how would you define the quality of service offered to them?

3. What do your competitors offer to customers which helps differentiate them from your organization?

4. What will be the benefits of being more customer-oriented for you and your department?

THE BUSINESS CASE

The business case for being a customer-oriented organization is powerful. By understanding customers' needs, updating that information through regular feedback, *genuinely* being interested in how they might want future products and services modified, an organization is able to establish a *sustainable* competitive advantage. At the *heart* of this competitive advantage lies not technology, not some super information system, but a belief that listening to customers, understanding their needs and basing business decisions on that information is critical for success.

Creating differentiation

In competitive markets where customers are spoilt for choice and products have the same features and benefits, what will differentiate your organization from the 'pack'? Many leading organizations, such as British Airways, Ford and Marks and Spencer have realized the commercial benefits of customer orientation. It is the quality of service, the rapport and relationship which is built with the customer which creates this differentiation.

Creating a differentiation through customer orientation is a people process. While your customer database might give you useful information on customers' buying preferences, how long ago they bought your products and when they are due for their next purchase, this is not enough to create the *perception* of differentiation in the eyes of the customer. Many buyers seek 'added-value' and do not buy purely on the basis of the cheapest price. If they *perceive* that company X has far superior service, delivery time and after-care than company Y, company X has created an important feature of differentiation. Needless to say, this perception must be backed up in reality.

It is worth noting that negative differentiation can be created too, if it is done on a regular enough basis. The banks and building societies, for example, entered the pensions and life assurance market in a big way, by being able to differentiate themselves from the life assurance companies through their 'clean' image.

Building understanding

Another feature of customer orientation and differentiation is the understanding which is gained through a long-term partnership. Customers can provide a lot of valuable information on buying preferences and what their future needs would be. By capitalizing on this understanding and getting close to the customer through quality of service, an organization will set its competitors a hard task gaining entry to its customers. *Understanding customers' needs and providing quality of service create a powerful side-effect: customer loyalty.*

Creating new opportunities

A third business benefit of being customer-oriented is that through understanding customers' needs, new opportunities are created. This is especially so with service organizations, which are ideally suited to creating new sales opportunities. This can be a very overt process, where customers are asked about the quality of service they received. If the response is positive, then it is not unreasonable to ask if there are other areas where your services could be used. If the response is negative, this is an ideal opportunity to put things right before the customer thinks about going to a competitor. The additional benefit of creating new selling opportunities is that you are *keeping competitors out* and your own selling costs are kept to a minimum.

PUTTING IT INTO PRACTICE

As a manager, what are the practical steps you need to take to improve customer orientation? The following are useful guides.

1. The need to measure current levels of customer satisfaction

The starting point in the drive to improve customer orientation is to find out what your customers think of you. Customers can provide invaluable information on how your organization is perceived, how it differs from competitors, and what they like and dislike about you. Getting to this stage, however, is not as simple as it may seem, for it presumes that you know who your customers are and that you can access them. For some organizations customers can be at numerous levels. Take for example, a manufacturer which supplies bathroom products to the building trade. Its products are retailed via builders merchants, bought by builders and installed in homes. In this case then, we have the *direct* customer (the builders merchants), the *indirect* customer (the builders themselves) and the *end user*. All three customers are inextricably linked, in that if the end user is not satisfied with the bathroom products – the taps leak, or do not work, for instance – they will not ask the builder to install the product in the future, and the builder in turn will not buy the products from the builders merchants. So, when we talk about understanding the levels of customer satisfaction it is important to be precise about whom we are referring to.

To further complicate the issue, there are *internal customers* who need to be satisfied too, for arguably, unless and until the needs of internal customers are being met, external customers will not get quality service. Each customer is also likely to have different needs and criteria, so make sure you understand what those are, rather than imposing yours on them. In the above example, the builders merchants might define their main need as timely delivery, while the builders themselves might require a range of products to suit different budgets, and the end user might want a reliable product which looks good.

The main factors which constitute customer satisfaction need to be translated into hard *performance targets*. In the case of the builders merchants, the performance standards might be to ensure that 98% of orders are delivered within 24 hours of the order being placed. Information from customers, then, is the starting point in identifying areas for improvement and setting clear performance targets.

2. Match products and services with customers' needs

This leads on to the next point, which is the importance of matching your own products and services with the needs of the customer. Customer orientation is about doing things which the customer wants and needs, rather than what is most convenient for you. In the process of meeting customers' needs, however, business needs must also be met. Take the example of extending bank opening hours – the expense of extending employees' working hours can be justified by more contact with customers, a greater number of transactions, gaining customer loyalty, not losing customers to competitors who are offering extended opening hours, etc.

It may be the case that meeting the needs of all customers is not possible with one product; a case for 'branding' then arises. Through branding, a company can tailor its core product to meet the needs of different customers. Still staying with our bathroom company, the brandings might potentially be: the 'budget' range to satisfy the needs of price-sensitive customers; the 'novelty' range for those who want a unique bathroom; and the 'luxury' range might provide gold fittings and other extras to the basic range.

Visit any major supermarket chain and you will see own-label products sitting alongside popular brand names – a response to losing customers to cut price stores such as Aldi, Netto and Kwik Save. If you specialize you risk narrowing down your customer base, while if you generalize, you risk not meeting the exact needs of any customer group. The positioning and targeting of products and services is a critical part of meeting the needs of different customer groups effectively.

3. Introduce service standards and innovations

Once you have defined who your customers are and what their various needs are, this information needs to be incorporated in the way you operate and do business. In other words, unless you define what exceeding customer expectations is, how will employees know what it means, how will they know how to achieve it and, more importantly, how will the business know that it is achieving what it has set out to achieve?

The introduction of *service standards* is often a start and end point for many organizations. These service standards can be like a long shopping-list: to ensure all phone calls are responded to after three rings; to go back to customers with a response after X minutes, etc. This is a very process-led service standard. A more proactive and dynamic system should, *in addition* to

41

this process list, encourage individuals to interpret service standards more personally, and be based around real-life success stories. By regularly communicating such stories, the importance of being customer-oriented becomes more than just empty words. In the case of the Marriott Hotel chain, they regularly feature customers' stories: for example, of a customer forgetting a briefcase in the hotel lounge on the way to the airport and only realizing this after the concierge had personally brought it to the airport; or having forgotten to bring some cufflinks for an important business lunch and being provided with the hotel manager's pair.

Customer orientation should also entail continuous improvements and innovations in levels of service. B&Q, for example, has fully-qualified electricians, bricklayers and plumbers employed as sales assistants in their larger stores; they run free 'how-to' demonstrations. The differentiation and 'added-value' are that they are one of the few national chains which can assist customers with their technical DIY requirements. In the case of the bathroom manufacturer I referred to earlier, its service innovation was to link its own computer system with the Electronic Point of Sale (EPOS) system used by its main distributors, hence having an instant record of what was selling and what was not, enabling production to be precisely geared to sales. In addition, they worked with the distributor on special promotions to sell the brands which were selling less well. Boots the Chemist has built an advertising campaign on the theme of 'Who cares enough to....?' and then goes on to list its products which take care of special requirements, for example cough medicines which do not cause drowsiness. Its innovation on this 'Who cares?' theme is to provide customers with a medical-data card (Medilink), which enables the pharmacist to check what medications have been prescribed for them in the past and therefore to have a much better appreciation of what over-the-counter medications may or may not be suitable.

In an article entitled 'Japan's Dark Side of Time', published in *The Harvard Business Review* (July–August, 1993), Stalk and Webber discuss the Akihabara district – Tokyo's (perhaps the world's) most advanced consumer electronics shopping centre. They describe the distinction in service offered by one store called Daiichi. Daiichi utilizes a powerful information system to store customer information and to link this to its core processes. When Daiichi customers buy a product, they get a three-year warranty instead of the standard one-year warranty supplied by the manufacturer. In view of the reliability of Japanese electronic products, very few actually fail in the first three years. So, at very little economic risk, it is offering its customers 'added-value' – a reason to shop with them rather than their competitors. For large purchases like refrigerators, customers get next-day delivery, while competitors generally take up to a week. The whole ethos of Daiichi is to serve the customer in every sense. They store customers' items which are 'out of season' (heaters and humidifiers in the summer for example), which is a useful service given the limited storage space in most Japanese homes. The innovations in customer service go further still. Near the end of the three-year warranty period customers get a phone call, offering to send a trained technician to check the item for problems before the warranty expires. In so doing, the technician is able to see what other products the customer has and which are likely to require replacement. This is fed back into the information system and analysed. When the time is appropriate a letter is sent out inviting the customer to view a new product, which would be an ideal replacement for the ageing model in the customer's home. More information on how leading organizations excel in meeting the needs of customers is given in Case History 2.2.

4. Creating a customer-centred business

Customer orientation can not be switched 'on and off' at will; it should be an attitude of mind in every individual. Being customer-oriented is about looking at what the organization does and 're-engineering' it to meet the needs of customers more efficiently and effectively. A company's ability to exceed its customers' expectations is only as strong as its weakest link. For some organizations that weak link is the way it is internally structured. Take the example of walking into a bank to enquire about a mortgage. You ask the information service desk for some information, take the literature and arrange to have a financial consultant come round. The consultant explores various options and leaves you with some choices. You then confirm with the consultant what your requirements are, fill in the necessary paperwork and await a response. In the meantime, the financial consultant hands your paperwork to the mortgage department, which then assesses how much of a risk you are. For many banks and building societies the bottleneck is the number of days it takes the mortgage department to turn around the paperwork. By the time you have had a response from the bank, numerous departments have had to be involved, which proves to be not only inefficient in terms of time and resources, but is not particularly customer-oriented. With the use of customer-oriented IT systems, and by re-engineering their internal processes, many financial organizations can deal with the individual at the branch or their homes (with the aid of 'lap-tops') and considerably improve the efficiency of getting a mortgage. In becoming more customer-oriented, many organizations are restructuring departments around key processes and not functional specialisms.

Being customer-oriented also means that internal policies need to consistently reinforce the message. The way that individuals are recruited, trained, developed, paid and appraised, needs to be consistent with what you are trying to achieve. Communication should provide regular information on customers' needs, what the competition is doing and feedback from customer satisfaction surveys. The bottom line is that commitment and conviction to excel in meeting customers' needs have to be regularly endorsed by senior managers. Unless they demonstrate customer-oriented behaviour – including the way they deal with their internal customers – little of any substance will be achieved. Case Histories 2.1 and 2.2 demonstrate how customer service can be dramatically enhanced by improving internal processes and linking it to job satisfaction and through better understanding the needs of customers.

THE KEY PRINCIPLES OF CUSTOMER ORIENTATION

This section looks at the key principles which lie behind effective customer satisfaction. These can be summarized under two main themes:

- the customer-supplier relationship
- your positioning on the 'expectation-perception' service model.

The customer-supplier relationship

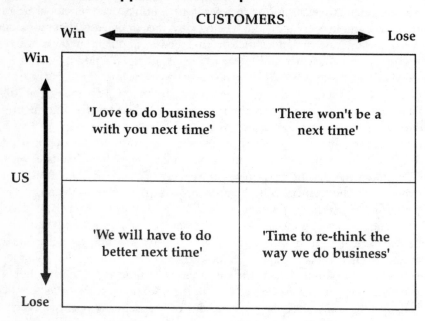

Figure 2.1 *Models of dealing with customers*

There is nothing radical or dramatic about the matrix in Figure 2.1. However, it does serve a purpose in helping you think about how customer-oriented you and your organization are. Being customer-oriented only comes about if the 'hearts and minds' of individuals and the organization as a whole are in tune with the belief that customers are *not a nuisance*. How many times have you been into a shop to be received with relative apathy and disinterest? How many times have you phoned up an organization to be passed from one individual to the next because it was not their area of responsibility? It is all too easy to get a 'them and us' mentality when you are dealing with customers. However, the sobering thought is that *no one wins* without a *win-win* outcome. A customer will not return for further business if they feel they have not had a good 'deal'. Taking it to its extreme, poor service with one supplier can have a knock-on effect on other suppliers – typified by our feelings about double-glazing and second-hand car salesmen. If a company loses out on a regular enough basis, it will go out of business.

If we consider suppliers as being part of the customer chain, the same theory and practice applies. Consider for example the car industry, where in a bid to cut their costs and improve profitability, some companies turn to their suppliers and try to negotiate lower prices for their products. However, this is the classic lose-lose scenario. If the suppliers feel that they are being exploited, they will try and cut corners through compromising on quality and/or buying cheaper raw materials. What some of the more forward thinking car manufacturers such as Toyota and Nissan have done is introduce their own project teams into suppliers. These project teams then work with suppliers to reduce costs and overheads, hence helping them maintain their profit margins while at the same time passing on savings to their customers. By going for a win-win outcome they are demonstrating their commitment to putting customers first.

Your positioning on the expectations-perceived service model

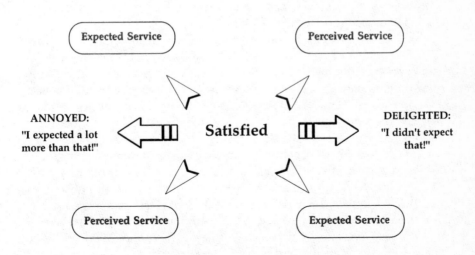

Figure 2.2 *A model of how to exceed customers' expectations*

It is important to understand and manage customers' expectations. The 'delight' of customers comes from their expectations being exceeded. Figure 2.2 highlights the importance of knowing what your customers' expectations are; without this information it would be difficult to knowingly exceed them. Customers' 'anger' arises from their expectations not being met. To create real differentiation through quality of service, new standards need to be continually set, so that expectations are always exceeded.

Case History 2.1

Is Competition the Only Route to Creating Better Customer Service? The Case of the Public Sector

In this chapter customer orientation has been talked of in terms of profitability, differentiation, competition and value to shareholders. How does this private sector model hold up in the public sector?

The government of the day has tried to ensure customer orientation is prominent in the public sector through the Citizens Charter and by bringing in market testing. But are market forces the only way to bring about customer orientation? There is no getting away from the fact that market forces are valuable in creating a paradigm shift, in shaking people from complacency and focusing the mind on providing quality service, because, 'if we don't, then others out there will'. However, this case history is intended to demonstrate how customer orientation can be brought about by making it an important feature of job satisfaction.

Take the case of the Housing Benefits Department of Halcyon City Council, which was concerned with the rising levels of assault against its employees by 'customers'. In addition it was concerned about the apathy from both employees and 'customers' on new customer initiatives, which invariably failed due to lack of ownership and commitment. The over-riding view amongst the council's employees was that the general public they came into contact with were a 'hassle-factor' they could well do without. They accordingly treated claimants with contempt and used various strategies to cope with this stressful environment. In other words, by being dispassionate, by being 'clinical' in the way they dealt with the general public, they were able to do their 9–5 without getting stressed. The stress was caused by this incongruence between *having* to deal with irate members of the general public all day long and *not* wanting to be in the 'front-line'. Members of the public were seen as being unreasonable, uncooperative, a nuisance and did not understand how the housing benefit systems worked. This ignorance led to unreasonable demands and behaviour, which they had to face. It was only through changing attitudes and behaviour that this 'lose-lose' cycle was broken.

In consultation with the Housing Department's employees, the following themes emerged: employees got job satisfaction from providing a quality service to customers; however, employees wanted greater autonomy and freedom in decision making rather than feeling they were operating on a production line. The root of the problem was *not* that employees did not like dealing with members of the public: it was the frustration of having to deal with angry claimants who had been 'pushed from pillar to post'. The housing team were facing the symptoms of an overloaded and inefficient system. By introducing more help-desks, help-lines and 'self-help' material, the council dramatically reduced the number of enquiries 'clogging' the system.

Here was a case then, where quality of service to customers was directly linked to job satisfaction. By removing the 'blockages' which prevented the provision of a quality service and enabling staff to achieve job satisfaction, a real impact was made in reducing the number of complaints made by claimants and the number of days council staff were taking off for sick leave.

Case History 2.2

Customer Orientation: Aspects of Success

What do organizations which are recognized as being 'best in their class' do in terms of customer service? The following are important factors:

- innovations in service
- innovations in technology
- innovations in after-care
- innovations in loyalty

Innovations in service

These organizations excel in the way they deal with customers and the level of service provided is of a very high standard. McDonald's has built its reputation on providing the same consistently high standard across the world. Its service standards in cleanliness, speed of delivery, cleaning litter in the vicinity of the shops and the 'have a nice day' have established it as a role model organization in this respect. Virgin offers its first-class business travellers courtesy chauffer-driven Range Rovers to the airport and to their destination at the other end. Marks and Spencer is renowned for being the first major retailer offering a 'no quibble money-back offer' on its products. BP and Texaco petrol stations offer customers shopping and eating facilities. With coffee machines, microwaves and other drinks machines, customers can eat on the move. IKEA offers baby-minding facilities to its shoppers. The supermarket giant Tesco offers facilities to mothers such as designated baby-changing areas. Birmingham Midshires Building Society offers to visit customers at home if they are unable to attend their branches.

Innovations in technology

For other organizations, technology enables them to stay one step ahead of the competition in providing superior customer service. Direct Line was the first insurance company to offer customers the convenience of being able to insure their car and home contents over the phone. Its parent company, the Royal Bank of Scotland, is also one of the few banks offering telephone banking: a system enabling customers to make transactions and enquiries on their accounts 24 hours a day over the phone. British Telecom's advances in optical fibres meant it can offer phones which enable you to see the person you are talking to. Federal Express provides its on-foot couriers in central London with data communications hand-held computers. In the tight security around the City following a spate of bombings, the collection and delivery of parcels by vehicles became very difficult. These hand-held computers enable the control centre to coordinate activities and maintain a high standard of customer service. Jaguar are developing engine diagnostic systems which enable service engineers to pin-point faults in their cars. With engine management systems becoming ever more sophisticated, Jaguar felt its service engineers needed more modern technology to provide customers with a quality service.

Innovations in after-care

For other organizations, excelling in customer care is also about the quality of after-care. This is typified by many Japanese car manufacturers, such as Mitsubishi offering a warranty on cars up to 100,000 miles or 6 years, whichever comes sooner. British Gas offers a servicing deal on central heating systems and gas appliances, which helps maintain its reputation as a quality operator in an industry beset with the problem of 'cowboys'.

Innovations in loyalty

Loyalty schemes can entail a number of innovations. British Airways offers Airmiles as an incentive, along with different benefits to its blue, silver and gold card holders. Other organizations such as Do It All offer to refund the difference if customers can purchase the same product cheaper anywhere else. In other words, if you shop with us we will reward you with added benefits.

Case History 2.3

Driving a Business by 'Exceeding Expectations': The Case of the Building Society

This case history is intended to demonstrate how impressive improvements in business performance can come about as a result of customer-driven change. Birmingham Midshires Building Society was named 'the most improved building society in 1993' by analysts from UBS stockbrokers. It was also voted No. 1 for service in the inaugural *Daily Telegraph*/First Direct Customer First Award in 1993, and in 1994 it won the 'Service Excellence Award' from Arthur Andersen and *Management Today*. Yet, only four years earlier Birmingham Midshires was a long way off from being a customer-oriented organization. Industry commentators in 1990 were describing it as one of the worst performing building societies and UBS analysts described it as in need of 'major surgery' to survive. While there is no doubt it has done more than survived – improving its performance from a top 20 building society in 1990 to a top 10 building society in 1994 – the real question is how it has achieved this position.

Under new leadership from 1990, Birmingham Midshires involved its teams in setting out a vision for the whole organization: 'By being FIRST Choice for our customers, people and business partners we will grow profitably.' Through being FIRST Choice – Friendly, Informal, Responsive, Service-oriented and Trustworthy – and re-engineering key processes to enable this, Birmingham Midshires began the first phase of the change process. A new customer satisfaction questionnaire process which has gathered feedback from over 500,000 of its customers was created to focus staff and business partners on putting the customer first. Key messages emerging from this mass of information are actioned by different project teams sponsored by senior managers. Exceeding expectations is the key theme of the Birmingham Midshires advertising campaign, and this is how it intends to differentiate itself from competitors.

Listening to staff views has also been critical in refocusing the organization to exceed customer expectations rather than just to satisfy them. A staff attitude survey team, made up of line operational people, sponsored by the director of HR, regularly tracks 'people opinion' and acts on their problems. The feedback process is managed by external consultants to preserve the anonymity of staff and the staff attitude team develop an action plan which is 'owned' by the executive team. The executive team ensure that any issues or barriers impeding the delivery of a high quality service to customers are addressed.

Birmingham Midshires Building Society has demonstrated how understanding the needs of customers and integrating internal processes to be geared to exceeding expectations can bring about real benefits to the bottom line.

KEY ACTION AND LEARNING POINTS

1. What have been the main learning points for you in this chapter?

2. What are the main steps you need to take to improve your levels of customer satisfaction, within what timescales and with what resources?

3. What attitudes and beliefs need to change in order for customer satisfaction to be more than just another process?

LEARNING POINTS FROM THE CASE HISTORIES AND PERSONAL VIEW

The government has introduced market forces into the public sector: creating NHS Trusts and introducing market testing into public services. The crusade is to achieve better value for money and to ensure customers get a better quality of service. The Halcyon City Council case history highlights that focusing on improving job satisfaction can be an important step in improving quality of service. By listening to the needs of customers and allowing people at the 'delivery-end' to have a far greater say in how those needs should be met, Halcyon found real improvements in customer service. In addition, by removing organizational barriers which were frustrating employees and preventing them from providing a quality service, Halcyon was ensuring that the improvements were enduring.

Case History 2.3 demonstrates the ways in which leading organizations provide excellence to their customers. Through matching the needs of customers with the skills and knowledge an organization has, service differentiation can be created.

SUMMARY

The business case

In a highly competitive business environment, organizations are looking for novel, more technologically sophisticated ways of creating differentiation. Differentiation is what gives organizations a competitive edge. The beauty of excelling in customer orientation is that there are many benefits. It is not easy to replicate. True customer orientation is a state of mind which needs to be ingrained in the very culture of the organization. It takes time, energy and commitment to create. Unless a competitor is serious in achieving a competitive advantage through customer service, they will more than likely fail. The commitment needs to start at the top and takes time to filter through the organization. Once achieved, however, the results are impressive. Customer orientation creates loyalty, and new opportunities for products and services to be sold. On top of all that, it dramatically reduces the cost of selling – customers come to you because they know what you are capable of and do not mind paying extra for peace of mind and quality.

Putting it into practice

There are several practical steps an organization can take to become more customer-oriented. The starting point has to be a review of what customers want and what they look for from their suppliers. Identifying who one's customers are is not as easy as it sounds, as there are direct customers, indirect customers and end users. Each level of customer influences the other. Identifying what customers want and how able you are to meet their needs provides a useful starting point. Having service standards and continuously introducing innovations in service levels are important too, sending out a clear message to customers that you are serious about winning their business and setting the standard others have to follow. While customer information is useful in targeting products, and service innovations make the buying process more convenient, the bottom line is that *quality of service itself* creates the lasting difference. By treating customers with integrity, providing quality advice and working for a win-win outcome, the best form of differentiation has been created – and one which is most difficult to duplicate.

The key principles

The key principles of customer satisfaction rest on two key themes: first, that the most beneficial type of customer/client relationship is the 'win-win' scenario. Successful organizations are always looking for ways in which they can add value to their products and services and view this as a vital means of building customer loyalty and keeping out competitors. Through the 'win-win' scenario successful organizations also dramatically reduce their selling costs – as customers are usually receptive to buying new products/services.

The second key principle relates to getting the right balance between the customer expectations and their perceptions of the service received. The challenge is ensuring that perceived service is always higher than customers' expectations – not easy, as expectations are continually improving.

Chapter 3

ANALYSIS AND DECISION MAKING

In particular, they (professionals) must learn how the very way they go about defining and solving problems can be a source of problems in its own right

(Argyris, 1991)

WHAT YOU CAN EXPECT

After reading this chapter, you will have a better understanding of:

■ why analysis and decision making are critical in management

■ the techniques available for better analysis

■ a structured process by which to analyse and reach decisions

■ the role of creativity in problem solving

■ why intelligent people are not always the best at analysing situations

■ how ineffective analysis leads to ineffective decisions

■ the principles underlying effective analysis and decision making

OVER TO YOU

1. What are the key issues you are currently trying to resolve in the work environment?

2. What is preventing you solving the issues – lack of information, resistance from others, being unclear on what to do?

3. What for you would be the ideal outcome: what would it feel like, how would it look and how would it be different from how things are now?

4. What positive aspects in the current situation could you incorporate in the new situation?

THE BUSINESS CASE

Analysis and decision making are *critical* at both the macro and micro levels if managers and organizations are to perform effectively. In today's rapidly changing market place, the need for constantly analysing and monitoring business trends is more critical than it has been in the past. In addition, the more senior a manager becomes, the more *weight and importance* is placed on a manager's ability to evaluate information and reach decisions effectively. This chapter deals with analysis and decision making synonymously for, all too often, a poor decision is preceded by shallow or incomplete analysis of a situation. So how and why are analysis and decision making important for the business? I have selected two main areas.

Managing the business processes

In a typical day, every manager will have to make numerous decisions based on a mass of information from a variety of sources. In managing the business processes – ensuring budgets and business plans are prepared; monitoring performance against these business indicators; ensuring work loads are evenly allocated; forecasting future requirements – a large degree of objectivity and analysis of data are required, along with the ability to reach decisions. This is what is sometimes referred to as 'single loop' learning – more of this in the Personal View 3.1.

Managing change

Analysis and decision making are also important in managing the 'softer' issues of change. Indeed, it could be argued that the quality and the nature of analysis and decision making required in managing change is dramatically different from that required in managing the business processes. Information is likely to be less tangible, to be from a far greater number of sources, and the consequences of decisions are likely to be far reaching. Indeed, the breadth and depth of analysis and decision making is a critical factor in the success or failure of change programmes. There is a growing body of evidence to suggest that bright, intelligent managers who are very able in dealing with complex financial data do less well when dealing with 'softer' business issues. For example, most mergers and acquisitions fail not for financial reasons but primarily because the integration of the two cultures and management teams had not been handled well. In other words, the pre-merger/acquisition analysis of 'hard' data is not followed through with adequate analysis and decision making on the 'softer' issues.

The bottom line is that the very survival of an organization depends on its ability to effectively collect business and market information, interpret it and then act on it. If these *skills* of analysis and decision making are inadequately performed, the consequences for shareholders, customers and the long-term future of the business are likely to be bleak.

PUTTING IT INTO PRACTICE

As a manager, what are the practical steps you need to take to effectively analyse situations and reach decisions?

Most managers are not taught how to solve problems systematically. Is it any wonder, then, that so much time and energy is often wasted through 'problems' being swept under the carpet or passed to someone else? After all, dealing with problems can be stressful and cause a great deal of inconvenience. A natural inclination is often to 'patch-up' a problem, so that the short-term need is attended to, rather than looking at the root causes of the problem. Any project team will tell you from bitter experience that it is much better to address problems at the start and get to the root of a problem, than deal with it at a later stage.

The 'golden rule of thumb' in business – that if things can go wrong they will – should be heeded. Unfortunately many managers often work on the assumption that they will be the exception or that they will be able to sort things out as they go along. The alternative view often quoted is, 'If it ain't broke, don't fix it'. This can lure managers into a false sense of security, that things are going well at the moment and there is no reason to think they will not continue to do so in the future. It is useful for managers to keep the model shown in Figure 3.1 in mind, which aligns problem solving with a project life cycle. The simple message is that as a manager you do not want to be tackling difficult issues and problems during the most critical phase of a project – the delivery.

An effective solution to solving problems is given in Figure 3.2. Indeed, this model is widely accepted as the standard four-step approach to analysis and decision making.

1. Analyse the problem

If you have a project or senior management team evaluating the *cause* of a problem, each member will have their own views and thoughts, ie speculations. Through analysing the problem the focus should move from *speculation* to tangible *evidence*. Take the example of a consultancy, which has found its order book quite dramatically tailing off towards the end of the year, having been extremely healthy at the beginning of the year. On getting the management team together to address the issue, the following are the types of comments around the table:

> There is a recession on out there and we are only just beginning to feel the effects; customers are getting far more cost sensitive and our prices are at the upper end of the market; there are other competitors creeping

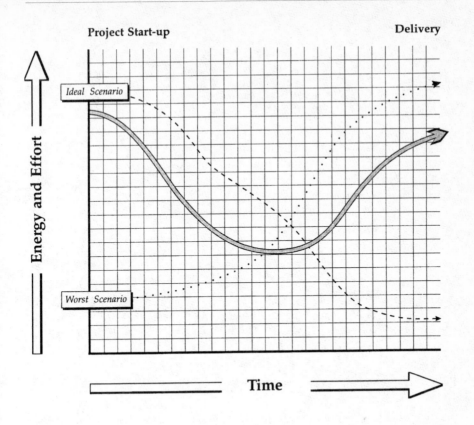

Figure 3.1 *Aligning problem solving with a project life cycle*

in to our market place and this is the first sign of them taking our customer base.

Potentially then, the problems facing this consultancy have multiplied from declining orders to a declining market place, warding off new competitors and competing on price. The *first* stage of analysing the problem, then, entails separating *cause* and *symptoms*. Here, the symptom of the problem is declining orders towards the end of the year. The cause is as yet unknown, although people have their own views as to why this is so. Analysing the problem requires more than speculation but getting as much useful and relevant data as

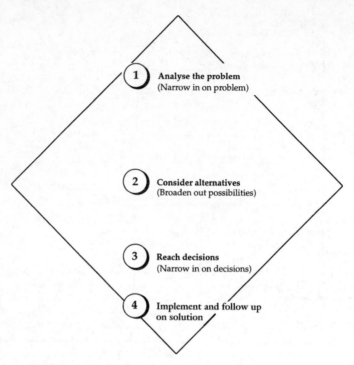

1. Analyse the problem
(Narrow in on problem)

2. Consider alternatives
(Broaden out possibilities)

3. Reach decisions
(Narrow in on decisions)

4. Implement and follow up
on solution

Figure 3.2 *An analysis and decision making model*

possible so that informed decisions can be made. In this case, the information analysed was:

- consultant workload
- where the business was coming from
- the variance in fees between the beginning and the end of the year.

The above data revealed an interesting trend: for the past six months, consultant workload had been incredibly high – in the majority of cases utilization (the amount of time doing client-facing work) was 100%. For the past two years, business had come 80% from existing clients, 20% from new clients. With existing clients, over 60% of the work had been generated by two consultants, through running client-facing events. The variance in fees from the first half of the year to the second half was approximately 20%. Analysing the situation revealed that the problem was *not* as 'life-threatening' as was first thought – a variance of 20% was 'survivable'. There was a logical explanation for the drop in workload towards the second half of the year: consultants were so busy delivering the work, they were not selling new work. In particular, given their reliance on repeat work, they were not maintaining the close relationships with the existing clients which they needed for this to materialize. Compounding the problem further was the fact that the two consultants who were bringing in over 60% of the fees were project-managing large assignments. The problem definition then was: *how can we manage the business, so that we even out the peaks and troughs of the consultancy work?*

2. Consider alternatives

There is often a temptation to go headlong and address the problem in the most convenient way, once it is clear what the cause of the problem is. In this model, the argument is that the most convenient method is not necessarily the best. Another temptation – and one you should really be careful to avoid (it happens so often) – is to evaluate an idea and declare it non-workable even before people have had a chance to consider it. It may be useful to get into the habit suggested by de Bono (1993): instead of saying an idea is ridiculous or it won't work, say what you like about an idea, what you dislike about an idea and most importantly how what has been suggested could be modified so that it might work. In this example, the following alternatives were put forward to address the problem:

- to have two teams of consultants, who rotate delivering and selling work;
- to employ a consultant dedicated to business development;
- to make greater use of associates who could be called in to manage the peaks, leaving other consultants to go out and win additional business;
- to encourage consultants to discuss new consultancy opportunities with clients they were currently working with;
- to have special 'time-outs' built into a consultant's diary, where they had to make time for marketing.

3. Reach decisions

This stage involves narrowing down the number of alternatives to those which will bring about the *desired results* most effectively. You can doubtless appreciate how difficult it would be to decide on the best option without being clear about the desired result. In the case we are discussing, the ideal result might be:

> to have an internal system which enables consultants to both deliver quality work to clients and sell new work, in order to sustain growth and profitability.

The key words in this ideal outcome are: *internal system, deliver, sell, growth* and *profitability*. Consultants should do both the selling and delivery of work, which reduces the attractiveness of hiring an external business development person. Growth would seem to make the option of using associates less attractive, while profitability narrows down the choice of alternatives in terms of the impact they will have on the bottom line. The focus would appear to be on getting the internal management system right, so that it then enables the other things to happen.

So, reaching decisions needs to be done against a set of *criteria*: an ideal outcome, the values of the organization and longer term business objectives.

These criteria are important to provide *a check*, that what is being proposed fits in with the general beliefs and values of the organization and does not compromise the longer term business objectives. This also ensures that 'poor' decisions are far less likely. A group can sometimes make 'impulsive' or 'consensus' decisions because they are the most convenient, or because they appear to be right – but they may not be the most appropriate. History is littered with decisions which, with hindsight, could have been different had they been 'validated' against clear criteria. Often the question: *'What are we trying to achieve here?'* focuses the mind on these criteria. The Conservative government has made several decisions which it has had to go back on: the poll tax is a classic example, for while it met the needs of the government, it did not meet the needs of the people it was intended to help. The introduction of a fairer system of taxation by the government was not perceived as such by the general public and, given that the general public were the key arbiters of whether this tax would be considered fair or not, it would not have been unreasonable to have included their requirements as part of the check-list.

The actual process of narrowing down the options also needs to be conducted sufficiently systematically, so that the group does not just gravitate to a 'natural' conclusion, because it happens to be the easiest or least painful. All the alternatives need to be given 'air-time' and chaired by 'an honest broker' – someone who will encourage the group to explore some less-obvious possibilities.

4. Implement and follow up

How many times have you been in a meeting where there is consensus on a particular recommendation (ie, there are no overt objections), but once out of the meeting there are 'rumblings' that the option will never work! If that was not bad enough, there are no milestones or monitoring systems in place to check that the interventions suggested are having the desired impact. Analysis is more than fault-finding and reaching a plan of action – it needs to be implemented too. Implementation requires the 'buy-in' of colleagues and team members; it requires their commitment to take on key responsibilities to ensure things actually get done. Consideration at this stage also needs to be given to potential 'barriers' outside the group. If you are working in a project group, there may be objections from people outside of the group who will be affected by your recommendations. It is as well to anticipate these and make contingencies.

THE KEY PRINCIPLES OF ANALYSIS AND DECISION MAKING

This section provides some information on the basic tools which a manager can use in creative problem solving. The intention here is not to provide an exhaustive list of problem-solving techniques, but to describe the range available. Before the different approaches are discussed it is worth noting that the approach you find helpful will depend on what *stage* of the problem solving process you are at. If, for example, you want *clarification* on what exactly the *nature of the problem* is, the technique you might want to use is an analysis interview; if you then want to *explore* the various options on how the problem might be addressed, then brainstorming might be appropriate; while in the final stage of clarifying a *course of action* 'force-field' analysis or the 'Pareto' principle might be appropriate. Let us look at these in turn.

Clarification of the problem

The *analysis interview* can be a very useful way to get a diverse range of information relatively quickly. The strength of this technique depends on the ability of the interviewer. Fundamentally, this technique is used to find out the scale of the problem at hand. Through interviewing job-holders, customers and 'experts', a manager is able to get a fix on the issues at hand. This approach is often used by managers with a wide-ranging problem to address, for example to improve profitability; to turn the company around; to improve the quality of a particular department's output, etc. To conduct an effective analysis interview the following points are suggested:

Prepare: it is important that the manager thinks through what areas he/she would like to ask questions on, how detailed the interview should be and the time they have available.

Manage the interview: it would be relatively easy to lose track of the interview and the main objectives without some structure. It is important to have a beginning, middle and end to the interview. The beginning could be an introduction from you on what you would like to achieve and how the interview will be conducted. Ask open ended questions: 'What are your views on... '; 'What are your suggestions on... '; 'Why is X done in the way it is... '. The middle part of the interview could be spent in narrowing in on key points: 'Tell me more about... '; 'Describe the way you manage your team... ', etc. The end of the interview usually consists of summarizing what has been said and clarifying any final points: 'So, if I understand it correctly, the way you manage your staff is primarily by... '; 'From what you have said, would I be right in thinking... '. As a general rule of thumb, the person being interviewed should be doing at least 80% of the talking.

Exploring options

Brainstorming is a useful way of getting quantity and quality of information on an issue relatively easily and within a short period of time. The basic principle is to focus attention on the main area(s) you want to explore further. It may be, for example, ways in which the company can more effectively market its products. It is important to make the group you are involving aware that you are after as many suggestions and ideas as possible – in fact you are positively encouraging them to come up with as many 'off-the-wall' ideas as they can. You are looking for spontaneous thoughts as they come, not measured, calculated responses. When ideas are being suggested, put them all on to a flip chart. Do not evaluate them or begin to censor some and include others. It is only when the group has exhausted all their ideas that you can begin to cluster them and make sense of the data you have. Again, when you are making sense of this information, involve the group in the process. It is important that people leave feeling it has been a worthwhile and useful exercise.

Focusing your attention on the most important issues

You are now at the stage where you have got so many ideas and so many potential areas you could usefully tackle that you need guidance on selecting the most important to focus your attention on. The *'Pareto' principle*, or the 80:20 rule, is one way to help focus your energies. The principle here is that 80% of an effect is caused by 20% of a variance; 80% of the sales are made by 20% of the sales people; 80% of the costs are down to 20% of the workforce. You can help your cause by focusing on the 20% that provide 80% of the opportunity for improvement.

Tackling a specific problem systematically

Force-field analysis is a useful technique in approaching a specific problem in a systematic way. Figure 3.3 details the usual layout of a force-field. The idea underlying the technique is that any situation has forces impacting on it: both 'enabling' and 'constraining' forces. In other words, in a change programme, an organization is likely to have a number of specific, definable objectives and there are factors which will both 'enable' and 'constrain' the objectives being achieved. Force-field analysis helps define what these forces are and encourages managers to think about how they can minimize or remove the 'constraining' forces, so that the organization will gravitate towards the desired objectives.

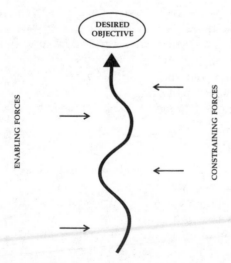

Figure 3.3 *A standard layout of a force-field analysis*

A Personal View 3.1

Do Intelligent People Analyse and Reach Decisions Most Effectively?

'That's a strange question to pose; I wonder what's behind it?' might be your first reaction when you read the title of this piece. This section is triggered by the work of Chris Argyris and his article published in *The Harvard Business Review* (May–June 1991). Argyris puts forward the concepts of 'single loop' and 'double loop' learning. The heart of his argument is that successful people are not often geared to learn from their own failures, because the strategies they use to problem-solve are limited. Behind 'single loop' learning is the principle of cause and effect: 'If I do X, then Y happens'. This is based on a scientific model and reinforced by teaching and education; in most cases it is effective. Hence intelligent people rarely experience failure.

To give you another example, consider a fictitious character called Sid, who works as a divisional manager for a pharmaceutical company. Sid's liked by his staff, is highly effective and runs a profitable department. His effectiveness rests on the fact that whenever his staff experience a problem good old Sid rolls up his sleeves and sorts the problem out. His knowledge of the industry, the department and his products, means that intuitively he can locate where the problem is, fix it and then hand back to the person concerned. In the majority of cases he is right. Sid was promoted to divisional director six months ago. He has the relevant managerial experience, track record and knowledge of the business; but why is Sid hating the job? A large part of the reason has to do with the fact that whenever a colleague approaches him with an issue or problem, Sid's tendency is to revert to type – 'let me show you what to do'. Many of the other divisional directors found this style highly patronizing at worst and paternalistic at best. They were somewhat taken aback by his style and quite a few felt he was interfering. From where Sid was standing he was doing his utmost to help out and all he got back was ingratitude. Sid's view that his colleagues were arrogant and opinionated was alienating him from them even further. In the words of Argyris:

> ... because (professionals) have rarely failed, they have never learned how to learn from failure. So whenever their single-loop learning strategies go wrong, they become defensive, screen out criticism, and put the 'blame' on anyone and everyone but themselves. In short, their ability to learn shuts down precisely at the moment they need it the most (*The Harvard Business Review*, May-June 1991, p. 100).

Double-loop strategies, however, enable managers to learn from their experiences and develop new models of thinking. Double loop learning encourages individuals to question their own effectiveness and, through insight, reach more flexible, innovative solutions.

The important lesson here is that analysis and decision making are far more complex processes than simply cause and effect – they are about changing 'single' strategy approaches of problem-solving to a multi-strategy approach.

Personal View 3.2

Common Problems in Problem Solving and Decision Making

Probably the one context where the inadequacy of problem solving and decision making is really highlighted for me is during meetings. Meetings form an important part of a manager's working life; they are time-consuming but are essential to the business. So what are the problems? I have highlighted four scenarios which are common at meetings.

Going round in circles

This is where members of a group are going round the same issues over and over again, but not adding anything to the debate. There are a number of factors which lie behind this scenario: the group are ill-prepared and therefore feel they can not address issues here and now. Perhaps the expectation is that someone else is more qualified to talk on this particular area and the group are feeling exposed. Or there is the feeling that this is such a major issue, and so contentious, no group member really wants to 'take the bull by the horns'.

Hidden agendas

This scenario is often linked to the previous one. It is characterized by a problem not being satisfactorily resolved because the group can not reach consensus. There is little enthusiasm or energy in the group because so many of the group members are keeping their cards close to their chest. The dilemma here is, 'How can we resolve this issue if I do not know what you are thinking and you are not prepared to tell me what you are thinking?'

Injured pride

This is often an outcome of the previous scenario. There are typically one or two 'brave soldiers' who diligently try to get to the heart of an issue. They provide ideas, suggestions and recommendations which are only halfheartedly received by the group. In disgust and despair these 'soldiers' tend to opt out, feeling they have been mistreated by the rest of the group.

Sweep it under the carpet

This is the culmination of the previous three scenarios. It is typified by no clear recommendations or action plans emerging. The group are keen to finish the meeting and are content to leave the issue to another day.

How can management meetings be made more effective? One of the interesting ideas put forward by Edward de Bono is that people in meetings should be encouraged to tackle issues and reach decisions in a more systematic way – which would allow many of the potential 'blocks' to meetings to be legitimately aired. He puts forward the concept of the six thinking hats:

White: the stage where the team deals with the facts and nothing but the facts.

Red: the stage where the team shares feelings, emotions, intuitions, prejudices and wishes.

Black: the stage where the team takes on the role of 'devil's advocate', discussing the negative aspects, threats and barriers to success.

Yellow: the stage where positive opportunities and strengths are discussed.

Green: the creative stage, where lateral thinking and new possibilities are explored.

Blue: the stage where decisions are made, where what the group is going to do is established.

The value of de Bono's six thinking hats is that they allow the group to constructively explore contentious issues wearing the red hat; or to be negative wearing the black hat. The focus though is on reaching decisions (the blue hat) through exploring creative opportunities (green hat) and positive thinking (yellow hat).

═══ KEY ACTION AND LEARNING POINTS ═══

1. What have been the main learning points for you in this chapter?

2. What are your strengths in analysis and decision making and how can you complement them, ie if you are usually very effective in objectively analysing data, could you complement this by exploring more creative ways of analysing a problem?

3. What are the new techniques you would like to acquire and practise; what timescales are you working to; what resources do you require? How will you check and monitor your performance? Who in the organization could you learn from?

Learning points from the personal views

The two personal views highlight how analysis and decision making play a critical part in a manager's life. In 3.1 the work of Chris Argyris is cited in connection with his theory on 'single-' and 'double-loop' learning. His contention is that professional people use a fairly narrow cause and effect model in problem solving. In solving most problems which have a clear cause and clear data supporting them, this style is very effective. This single-loop strategy is less effective in situations which require self-analysis and learning from situations. Where managers experience failure in solving interpersonal problems and other 'soft' problems, Argyris contends that they are likely to resort to denial or defensive behaviour. Double-loop learning provides managers with a wider model with which to analyse and learn from situations.

SUMMARY

The business case

The ability to analyse business and market information and reach decisions which have taken into account the relevant issues are a feature of effective managers and organizations. It is important that managers give the same importance to 'soft' business issues as that given to 'hard' issues. While the analysis of 'hard' data is often reliant on the logic of cause and effect, dealing with the 'soft' issues requires a much broader and fluid thinking style. Smart analysis and decision making prevent having to 'firefight' and patch up problems later.

Putting it into practice

Managers are not often taught a systematic approach to problem solving. This section looks at a four-step model which encourages managers to focus on analysing the nature of the problem at hand. Focusing on the cause of the problem rather than the symptoms provides a much clearer picture on where energy and resources need to be channelled. Once the problem has been clearly analysed, managers need to consider the alternatives available to them. Considering all the alternatives ensures that managers are not taking the easiest or most convenient option. The objective of this stage is to explore the options which will provide the optimum benefit. Narrowing the options down requires a precise definition of the optimum scenario. This then provides a 'template' against which options can be validated. The final stage of the four-step process is the implementation of the solution. This requires appreciating what the potential barriers to effective implementation are, having monitoring mechanisms in place and responsibilities assigned to different team members.

The key principles

The effective analysis of problems and decision making is considerably enhanced by a number of techniques. The most relevant techniques will depend on which part of the analysis and decision making process you are at. In the clarification stage, the analysis interview enables a manager to gather relevant information fairly quickly. In then exploring various alternatives, brainstorming can prove highly effective. The 'Pareto' principle and 'force-field' analysis focus attention on the most critical areas to tackle and what enabling and constraining forces need to be considered. Not surprisingly, one of the more innovative ideas is suggested by de Bono and his six hats principle, which recommends that teams should go through different processes of analysing a problem for the most effective decision to be reached.

Section 2

INFLUENCING AND PERSUADING OTHERS

S = Software contains a questionnaire relevant to this area

Chapter 4

INTERPERSONAL COMMUNICATION

*He was tough but fair ... he would listen to you – even when he was
dressing you down, he never left you feeling smaller. He might totally
take you to the bone, but he would build you up.*

(Nayak and Ketteringham, 1993)

WHAT YOU CAN EXPECT

After reading this chapter, you will have a better understanding of:

■ the key features of interpersonal communication

■ communication strategies

■ the value of interpersonal communication in business

■ how what you say is as important as how you say it

■ the barriers to effective interpersonal communication

■ the characteristics of effective communicators

■ how to improve your interpersonal style

OVER TO YOU

1. What are the most common situations where you are required to communicate with others? (eg meetings, presentations, sales meetings)

2. In which aspects of your communication style are you effective, and in which less effective?

3. From the Job Profiler, how important is interpersonal communication for the role you have? What does this tell you?

4. From the Self-insight Questionnaire is this an area of strength or development? What conclusions can you show from this self-assessment?

THE BUSINESS CASE

Every facet of organizational life relies on interpersonal communication. The business world could not exist without people communicating with each other person-to-person. Meetings, interviews, discussions, debates, selling and managing are all reliant on two or more people exchanging views and information. We all communicate for the majority of our working lives and no doubt take this skill for granted. It is when things go wrong: when sales opportunities are lost, when client relationships get soured, when projects begin to go off the rails, that we realize the importance of interpersonal communication. Effective interpersonal communication is just as much an asset for an organization as technical and business skills and is vital for the effective functioning of a business. This section highlights just two areas to demonstrate the value of interpersonal communication to the bottom line.

Selling

The survival of every profit-making organization depends on its ability to sell its products/services. Selling is fundamentally reliant on several key features of effective interpersonal communication, for example: *understanding* what the other person's needs are; *listening* to what they say; using appropriate *body language* and *eye-contact* to demonstrate you are interested in hearing what they have to say and that you are keen to know more about their business.

You in turn will match the features and benefits of your products/services with the needs of the client. You may well ask *questions* or *seek clarification* on several points and all the while try to evaluate whether the client's *language, tone of voice* and *body language* are conveying 'buying signals'. The client's interpretation of your interpersonal style is that you are someone they can *relate to*, they see you as *friendly*, as someone who is professional and knows the products/services you are selling. In this brief example the salesperson has formed the basis for a potentially fruitful long-term business relationship: a relationship which is based on two individuals who are able to establish a rapport, are able to make themselves understood and feel comfortable negotiating with each other. In short, effective interpersonal communication is vital for any organization which relies on sales people going out into a highly competitive market place and winning business.

Managing the business

The efficient functioning of a business relies on effective interpersonal skills. Imagine the following 'worst scenario' of a manager who is insufficiently sensitive to the needs of others, to the extent that he upsets people and is seen as 'adding fuel to the fire' with his lack of tact and judgement. At meetings he constantly talks without allowing space for others to do so and when they do he frequently interrupts them. His colleagues have noticed how he seems to 'switch off' when someone else is trying to make a point, only to then take-up his own point of view as soon as they have finished. Problems are caused by staff wanting to move from his department because they feel they can not relate to him, while new appointees seem to move on within six months. Customers too, have regularly asked for someone else to deal them; they complain that he does not attempt to understand their requirements and when things do go wrong – a late delivery for example – he will blame the client for giving insufficient notice. In short, without good interpersonal skills managers could not perform their role effectively – after all, the way others relate and respond to you determines your credibility.

Interpersonal communication is often taken for granted, as it forms such a fundamental part of our private and working lives. Perhaps this is why we rarely stop to question how effective we are. However, much of our effectiveness depends on how others perceive and relate to us. Good interpersonal skills mean that deals can be clinched, customers feel they want to work with you; internal colleagues regard your interpersonal style as a valuable asset in ensuring meetings run smoothly, and subordinates feel you are someone they can talk to about resolving problems and conflicts.

PUTTING IT INTO PRACTICE

As a manager, what are the steps you need to take to ensure your interpersonal communication is effective? You may find the following a useful guide.

1. Communicate objectively, not in emotionally charged language

Handling sensitive issues is something most managers would have to do on a daily basis: individuals who are under-performing; a project which is being poorly managed and is running behind schedule and exceeding budget; or two individuals who have difficulty working together. There is no reason why dealing with individuals in these scenarios in face-to-face meetings should not result in successful outcomes.

The first golden rule of effective communication is: make it objective. By being objective you are avoiding the deadly error of 'shooting yourself in the foot' – sitting in judgement on others and laying the blame at their door. In the case of the person who is under-performing, it would be easy to say: 'You've got a problem; unless you get your act together and sort yourself out, you'll be out of here pretty quickly'. The more effective communicators, however, focus on the problem itself, rather than the person and, in so doing, reduce the emotional charge of the situation. Their response to the above situation would be something along the following lines: 'How would you rate your own performance on these various assignments?... So, you're saying things could be dramatically improved. What can we do, therefore, to ensure the same problems do not arise in the future... ?' In this example the communicator has asked an open, non-threatening question and then used the person's own words to summarize the situation. This is followed by another open-ended question which, by incorporating the word 'we', sends the message: I would like to help you, by working with you, not by telling you what to do.

2. Express yourself genuinely

Effective interpersonal communication is about ensuring you get your point across in a way which is open, non-threatening and is understood by the receiver in the way you intended. This is the essence of what being genuine means. There are a number of points which need to be drawn out from this sentence.

First, what is meant by being 'open'? Being open is about making it clear to the other person what your agenda is. It means the person receiving your message is not trying to read between the lines to figure out why you may be saying what you are. In the case of the under-performing colleague, being open means saying something like: 'I think I know you well enough to know that you can perform a lot better and I would like to help you resolve whatever problems or concerns you may have. Are you willing to let me do so ... ?'

The importance of being non-threatening is that it does not put the other person on the defensive. Given that interpersonal communication is a two-way process, the most effective way to get the other person's cooperation is by making them feel you genuinely mean what you say. Through open, joint discussion there is far less likelihood of your message being misunderstood or misinterpreted by the other person. (Refer to Case History 4.2 for more on how your communication style is just as important as what you say.)

3. Use 'I' language not 'they' language

For interpersonal communication to be effective, it is important to make communication personal with the use of 'I' language, eg, 'I feel; I think; I would like ... '. The use of 'I' makes it very clear to the other person exactly where you stand and is an important feature of being 'congruent': meaning what you say. The 'they' scenario is a classic 'disowning' tactic. 'They' are often used as a scapegoat to mask what the person's own intentions are. How often have you heard a manager or colleague say: 'They asked me to tell you ... ; they said they could not go ahead with your plan because ... ; they want you to improve performance levels, otherwise they want you out'. If you want to convey a difficult message and genuinely want to bring about a desired outcome, use the 'I' language: 'I feel you can dramatically improve your performance and this is what I think and feel and this is how I can help ... '. This type of approach sends the message that you personally care, that you are personally involved and that you want there to be no ambiguity about what you think and what you say.

4. Listen attentively

Effective interpersonal communication is not just about sending out information, but also about receiving it. Listening, therefore, is a critical ingredient in communication. Attentive listening sends the following messages to the other person: 'I consider what you have to say as being sufficiently important that I am willing to sit and try to understand what your point of view is. I am further endorsing this by allowing you to say what you want, in your own way, in your own time and as fully as you like. Through attentive listening I am also sending the message that I would like to be supportive and am prepared to be persuaded by what you have to say, without pre-judging you'.

Given that negotiations, meetings, performance appraisals, interviews, etc. all revolve around sharing information and reaching a mutual understanding, effective listening is an important aspect of interpersonal communication.

5. Seek to make communication a two-way process

Individuals rarely do without a reason, and it is important that you try and understand the thinking behind the actions. Problems occur when you try to interpret events using your model of the world, rather than trying to see them through the eyes of the other person. Communication can be used inappropriately as a source of power: a means of putting the other person down.

As a manager, one of your responsibilities is to resolve problems which impede the efficient functioning of the business. The focus on achieving a successful outcome should gear the communication to the future, not to the past, and therefore be far more likely to bring about two-way discussion. The under-performing team member, for example, may have personal concerns, unrelated to work; but you need to establish that before you can begin to start addressing the performance issues. You can not after all force the team member to improve their performance; in any case you would be addressing the symptoms not the cause, thereby increasing the chances of the problem re-recurring in some other way. It is only through making communication a two-way process that meaningful decisions can be reached, with all the facts and information having been taken into account.

6. Look for feedback, without being prescriptive

Another way of ensuring communication is a two-way process is to test out your ideas and views with others, so that your understanding of things matches theirs. Apart from anything else this demonstrates equality in communication – not superiority. This equality is a far more effective way for a manager to improve performance, by checking that the person whose cooperation is most required is happy with the plan of action. Feedback enables 'fine-tuning' to take place and dramatically increases the chances of a successful outcome. You decide which of these two scenarios is likely to be most effective:

– John, following our discussions I have some thoughts on how your work perfor-
mance can be improved, but I would like to get your views on them first....
– John, I've heard what you have to say, you have shown yourself to be irrespon-
sible, and you leave me with no alternative but to tell you what you must do to
improve your work performance.

7. Be precise and do not generalize

How many times have you come across people who, by generalizing, manage
to 'switch-off' the person they are talking to? 'You're always late; you're always
obstructive; I might have known that as usual you would say something
confrontational' – are just some examples of generalizations. By generalizing
we label others. Others in turn are far more likely to generalize and label us
too: 'I've noticed how you always criticise others' ideas... ; you always have to
have the last word at meetings, which undermines others' contributions'. The
end result is that both parties get defensive and the value of the communication rapidly degenerates.

Generalizations can be described as 'red-flag' effects, serving to 'enrage'
others and dramatically reduce the power of what you have to say. By being
precise, on the other hand, you are being non-confrontational and getting the
other person's attention by having facts to hand:

> In that meeting you used language such as 'I must... ' and 'I want... ' on
> some ten to 15 occasions. You came across as very assertive – were you
> aware of that? I noticed that the more you were saying what you wanted,
> the more defensive other group members were becoming. Ann, for
> example, hardly made eye contact with you and made few contributions
> after the first ten minutes. I think you are far more effective when you....

This short dialogue demonstrates three benefits in being precise: the problem
is *clearly defined*; the *consequences* of the problem are described; and more *alter-*
native approaches can be discussed. Case History 4.1 describes the problems
which can arise from failing to be precise about others' work performance.

8. Discuss shared agendas, not own agendas

Finally, effective interpersonal communication is about having shared agendas,
where both parties are getting benefit and meaning from the interaction.
Communication is a powerful means of getting what you want and consequently is open to abuse. One of the most common ways it is abused is where
an individual has their own 'political' ends. Irrespective of what others want
they will keep bringing the conversation and meeting round to their own
agenda. Politicians in particular tend to be very adept at avoiding direct
questions and being 'immune' to discussing problems and issues which are
relevant to others. A meeting of five individuals, each with their own separate
agenda, will not achieve anything constructive. It is important to know what

the open and hidden agendas are, so the meeting can be managed to achieve a successful outcome.

THE KEY PRINCIPLES OF INTERPERSONAL COMMUNICATION

Interpersonal communication is about the effective exchange of information between two people. The work on this subject matter is extensive and can be broadly described under the following headings:

- dynamics
- purpose, and
- style

The dynamics of communication

Understanding the dynamics of communication helps convey how communication is a two-way process, between the sender (the person wishing to convey something) and the receiver (who becomes open to the reception of information). An important contribution to this field is made by Eric Berne (1972) and his work on transactional analysis. The premise of Berne's work is that each individual continuously interacts with the world in one of three states: the adult, child and parent. Our communication style and the way we interact with others will differ depending on our state. The parent state contains the values and morals we have been taught. It contains our standards for living and enables us to say what is right or wrong. The adult state is the rational, unemotional way we behave, which deals with the reality of what is actually happening. The child state contains the emotions and feelings. What is interesting, then, is the way people who are in different states interact. Take for example the following interactions between a manager and their subordinate:

Manager: John, your performance over the past two weeks has been abysmal, what on earth has got into you?

Subordinate: I'm really sorry, I have been under a lot of pressure in the past month. It won't happen again.

The manager is in the parent state, criticizing performance in very general terms and treating the subordinate as a child. The subordinate responds from their child state and indirectly agrees their performance has been abysmal. A conversation with both people in the adult state, on the other hand, might be something like the following:

Manager: John, in the report you submitted last week, where did you get the sales figures from ... are you sure they are the most up to date?
Subordinate: I got them from last month's sales report. I'll check with Liz, the sales director, to see if she has any more updated information.

Here both manager and subordinate deal with the accuracy of the sales information in a very rational, matter-of-fact way.

The purpose of the communication

In any interpersonal communication the needs of both parties have to be met. Unless expectations are understood and the 'ground-rules' on the purpose of the meeting are clear, the end result will be confusion. Take the following example:

> A wants to chat informally to B, who has specialist technical expertise about a work-related problem; B, however, thinks A wants specific information on how to address his problem. Both are coming to the meeting with different needs and expectations. B dominates the meeting, leaving A feeling somewhat confused and 'shell-shocked'. B interprets A's unease as confirmation that A is 'out of his depth' on this skill area and therefore tries even harder to make sure he gets his points across.

Many different types of behaviour in interactions – aggressive, passive, manipulative and assertive – can be attributed to this mismatch of expectations and needs.

The communication style

Different communication styles are appropriate depending on the purpose of the communication and the desired outcome. How information is communicated is as important as what is communicated. The main communication styles can be described as:

> *telling*
> *advising*
> *counselling*
> *consulting, and*
> *coaching.*

Telling: this style is most appropriate where others want specific guidance and information. It excludes others from the interaction and focuses on delivering information. It is most appropriate in a 'trouble-shooting' role, where others need no-nonsense, direct information.

Advising: this style is most appropriate where others want assistance from an expert or someone who is deemed to have skills in a particular area. The advising style is most appropriate when others do not want to be told what to do, but need guidance and 'hand-holding'.

Counselling: this is a non-directive style, where people solve issues for themselves through the insight the counsellor is able to provide. The style is facilitative and non-judgemental. It is most effective when dealing with individuals on a one-to-one basis.

Consulting: process consulting is most effective when others perceive they require your skills and expertise. This style is most effective in getting people to reach their own solutions (through your consultative skills), as they will be implementing them when you are not on the scene.

Coaching: this is most effective where others are aware of the issues and problems at hand and may have decided on the course of action they want to take. They need someone to help them through the change process, who can do so in a non-directive manner. Coaching is most effective in helping others to learn from past events, so they are better able to help themselves in the future.

Case History 4.1

What are the Most Common Problems in Interpersonal Communication?

This case history highlights some of the main issues to do with interpersonal communication. Some months ago I was asked to assess a manager, whom his employers felt they had a problem with. Having been the manager of a large department, he was demoted after only six months back to a specialist function. The manager had been with the company for over 20 years and had valuable technical expertise which the company recognized. The manager felt he had been unfairly treated by the company and had lost face by being demoted so quickly. He put it down to a number of 'trouble-makers' who had it in for him and reported every point they disagreed with to his boss. His boss saw it differently, however; he felt Keith (not his real name) had been promoted beyond his capabilities. Keith, he argued, was not a people-person; he was too shy and reserved and would not willingly communicate with others. He keeps himself to himself and locks himself away in his office. He won't even go to the staff refectory until late in the lunch hour so that he will avoid having to communicate with people. When he does speak, he has no tact at all; he gets people's backs up.

Keith's story was different. I did find him to be a shy person, but he was quite open and frank with his views. He saw his main fault as being a 'non-political' manager; he said what he thought and he felt other people disliked him for it. He did not see that other people found him aloof and difficult to talk to, a point he described as 'nonsense'. The bottom line was that how Keith saw himself and how others saw him were dramatically different. Due to what Keith felt were constant 'attacks' on him by others, he became even more defensive in his communications and refused to accept the others' point of view. He focused more on 'protecting his back' than listening and trying to understand the others' perspective. His defensive behaviour got to the stage where he refused to accept anybody's point of view – it was his way of coping and responding to others refusing to accept his own views.

It was only through objective assessment and feedback from colleagues, peers and non-work related associates that he accepted his communication style was ineffective, born of insecurity and a perceived threat from others. Keith's interpersonal difficulties resulted from a lack of self-confidence, caused by six months of criticism of his management style. Not unnaturally, his coping strategy was to avoid the situations which caused the distress – the people he managed. Keith admitted that he would do anything to avoid coming into contact with others; he saw himself as a target for others to unload their problems and he could do without that. As time went on he had difficulty maintaining eye contact with others, who interpreted this as yet another sign of poor interpersonal skills. When others were talking to him, his mind would be working overtime, trying to figure out what hidden agenda they had. Not surprisingly, he was described as having 'selective' hearing – hearing what he wanted to and blocking out the rest. It was only with Keith admitting that his interpersonal style caused problems and addressing the reasons behind this, that he was able to improve the way he communicated and interacted with others.

Case History 4.2

It's Not What You Say but the Way That You Say it ...

How true and accurate is the statement: 'it's not what you say but the way that you say it'? In my role as an occupational psychologist I have run numerous leadership development programmes for people who are deemed to be 'high-fliers'. An important element of these programmes is to provide individuals with feedback on areas of strengths and development needs. Candidates are often asked to give a presentation or an exercise, where the individual is required to get a message across and get the commitment and 'buy-in' of their audience. The background information candidates receive is always the same; they are on a 'level playing field'. So why do some candidates perform better than others? From my own experience, some of the difference rests on better analysis and understanding of the information. By far the biggest factor which differentiates the more effective from the less effective candidate is their style of interpersonal communication. In the majority of cases the information which is communicated by candidates is similar. The more effective candidates, however, excel in the following ways:

Setting the scene: those that excel in interpersonal communication ensure the recipient of their message is fully aware of what they are going to say, how long the meeting will take and check whether it is in accordance with the receiver's understanding of the meeting. This has the effect of ensuring both are talking to a shared agenda and with a shared objective.

Involving the receiver: setting the scene also has the benefit of actively involving the receiver. Communication is after all a two-way process and if the objective is to get a message across to the receiver it is important that both receiver and sender are involved in a joint process, where points can be clarified, issues can be resolved and, psychologically, the receiver feels they have been 'sold' to rather than 'told'.

Gaining commitment: very rarely does communication in business require passive acceptance on the receiver's part; some activity or momentum is required from the receiver, as a result of the communication. Any follow-up action requires commitment from the receiver, which can only come about once their commitment has been secured.

Establishing rapport: a communication style can be said to be effective if a message is tailored to have the desired impact on a particular audience. If in a negotiation I do not treat the other person equitably, or deal seriously with their concerns and make the other person feel uncomfortable, I will not establish a rapport and consequently the negotiation will be seriously flawed.

Coming across as genuine: the psychology of communication is such that if I feel the other person is insincere or their style of delivery is incompatible with the actual message, I will not take their message seriously.

Incongruence – where what is said is not supported with appropriate body language – is a major block to effective communication. In short, what you say and the way that you say it are equally important.

KEY ACTION AND LEARNING POINTS

1. What have been the main learning points for you in this chapter?

2. How will you apply the key learning points to the issues you are currently facing? What timescales are you working to and what resources do you require?

3. What do you need to do to improve your interpersonal effectiveness? How have others described your strengths and weaknesses in the way you relate to and communicate with others?

LEARNING POINTS FROM THE CASE HISTORIES

Case History 4.1 highlights how interpersonal communication is strongly influenced by the perceptions 'players' have of themselves and others. In this example a newly-promoted manager was deemed to be ineffective by his staff because they felt he was aloof and did not have the interpersonal skills they would expect of a manager at his level. He in turn became quite defensive about the comments made about him – inevitably, behind his back or indirectly. His coping strategy was to distance himself even further from his staff, only serving to confirm their fears even further. The reality is that effective interpersonal style is in the eye of the beholder.

The second case history identifies the key features of managers who are deemed to be effective in their interpersonal style. In the main, effective communicators ensure that they take their 'audience' with them and actively involve them in interactions. They check that the rationale behind key messages is explained and is understood by the receiver. They communicate with confidence, are deemed to be sincere and use a communication style which is most appropriate to the level of the audience.

SUMMARY

The business case

Interpersonal communication is a critical managerial skill, which is essential for the effective functioning of an organization. In both internal and external aspects of the business, communication skills are key. Internally, for example, managers who are insensitive to the needs of others and are unable to handle conflict and relate well with others, would soon cause major difficulties for the business. Equally, an organization whose managers are unable to relate well with customers and are unable to clinch deals because they do not build a rapport and empathy with others would soon be facing severe difficulties.

Putting it into practice

Effective communicators handle problems by focusing on the task, rather than the people performing the task. They focus on being constructive and putting things right, not on apportioning blame. Their effectiveness rests on a number of key steps. They come across as sincere and genuinely interested in wanting to work with others. They try and understand others' points of view by asking open-ended questions and listening attentively. By being non-judgemental, working to shared agendas, and being precise in the way they provide feedback to others, effective communicators can resolve people-related problems quickly and efficiently.

The key principles

Effective interpersonal communication can be enhanced by understanding a number of key principles: the dynamics of communication, the needs of the parties involved and the communication style which will have the desired impact. Understanding the dynamics of interpersonal communication is important for it provides some insight on why others say what they do and react they way they do. Berne's work on transactional analysis is important in this area. By understanding the needs of the person you are communicating with, you are able to ensure you are not talking at 'cross-purposes' or indeed unnecessarily confusing and complicating the interaction. Understanding what the other person's needs and wants are will also help in determining the most appropriate communication style. How things are said is as important as what is actually said.

Chapter 5

INFLUENCING AND PERSUADING OTHERS

Influential people have power, but not all powerful people have influence
Whetten and Cameron, 1991)

WHAT YOU CAN EXPECT

After reading this chapter, you will have a better understanding of:

- influencing strategies

- how influencing and persuading are linked to 'power'

- how effective influencers influence

- how what you want will determine your influencing strategy

- practical steps to influence effectively

- why and how to play for 'win-win' outcomes

- knowing your power – knowing your influencing style

Refer to the software for an insight into your influencing style.

——— OVER TO YOU ———

1. What are the main situations where you need to influence and persuade others?

2. What aspects of influencing do you consider yourself to be effective in and which areas less effective?

3. What conclusions can you reach from the Self-insight Questionnaire and how does this compare to the Job Analysis Questionnaire?

4. How important do you consider influencing and persuading to be for any future positions?

THE BUSINESS CASE

At major objective of every commercial organization is to *influence and persuade others* to buy their products or services. From advertising to individual negotiations the name of the game is to show why and how your company and your products are better than the competition's. Most organizations need to influence and persuade three distinct audiences:

- the City and financial backers
- customers
- employees.

The City and financial backers

The perception this group has of your company is critical if you are to have sustained growth and profitability. Arguably the best relationship between financial backers and a company is a loose partnership, where each has the best interests of the other at heart, without becoming too intrusive. Unfortunately, in the majority of cases the reality is very different. Financial backers tend to leave companies to 'do their thing', until they feel the company is in trouble. A company facing difficult times needs to have the ability to *influence and persuade* its financial backers; it could mean the difference between success and failure in gaining approval for a major loan for expansion, capital expenditure, acquisition, etc. Ultimately a company's share prices are strongly influenced by the City's *confidence* in it, and gaining this confidence is strongly associated with a company's ability to influence and persuade the City of its strategic, managerial and financial viability.

Customers

Winning customers and retaining existing customers is strongly related to the skill of influencing and persuading them. The value of market research is that it enables companies to target their influencing tactics to have the greatest impact on their chosen audiences. Selling, therefore, is the final outcome in the influencing and persuading process. Organizations who are effective in selling do so by identifying the needs of customers, meeting them with a product/service and then influencing them to buy their products/services through various strategies.

Employees

For business goals and objectives to be achieved, it is essential that employees are fully involved and committed. To gain the required commitment, organizations can influence and persuade employees through involving them in the decision-making process and providing them with the training and support they require to implement the decisions they reach. Receiving regular 'bottom-up' feedback provides continuity to the influencing cycle.

======= PUTTING IT INTO PRACTICE =======

What should you, as a manager, be doing at a practical level to influence and persuade others? Whether effectively selling to clients or persuading and influencing internal customers or colleagues in a meeting, there is a seven-step approach (shown in Figure 5.1) which you may find useful:

1. Define your objectives.
2. Understand the 'influencee's' wants and needs.
3. Prepare your ground.
4. Involve the influencee(s).
5. Positively sell the benefits.
6. Clinch objectives and then 'get out'.
7. Ensure prompt action is taken on decisions.

1. Define your objectives

It is imperative that before going into a negotiation you are clear what you want to get out of it. Being clear is not just having an idea of what you would like to achieve, but firm, tangible objectives. It is also useful to clarify what the 'best' and 'worst' scenarios might be, so that you have some idea of the parameters. Remember, in influencing and persuading others, you are always dealing with moving goal-posts: either the other party's agenda changes, circumstances change or the needs of both parties change. Defining your objectives helps you not to lose sight of what you are trying to achieve. It is conceivable that a negotiation changes so dramatically, with new information or changing needs, that your original objectives no longer apply. Under such circumstances, it is advisable to arrange another meeting, consider the facts and information you have before you and redefine your objectives or at least clarify them. Without a clear idea of what you are trying to achieve, you will be taken along a roller-coaster ride which you are not in control of. *Defining your objectives is about taking control.*

2. Understand the influencee's wants and needs

In any negotiation, meeting or debate there are often several agendas, either overt or covert. To influence and persuade the person you are trying to 'win-over', it is important to understand their needs and wants. The more overt needs are easy enough to establish: you can simply ask the person about their main needs and requirements and then seek to match what you are offering to their requirements. The more covert needs, however, are less easy to identify. This you will have to do through understanding the 'language' used and the clues the other person provides. Let me give you an example:

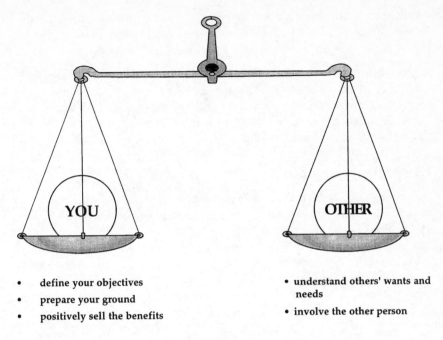

- define your objectives
- prepare your ground
- positively sell the benefits

- understand others' wants and needs
- involve the other person

- agree objectives
- ensure prompt action

Figure 5.1 *Getting the balance right in influencing and persuading*

A colleague and I recently presented to a life assurance company which wanted managerial assessments of their sales people. As a psychologist, assessment is quite a routine part of my job, but it is important to clarify why the client wants the assessment done in the first place – after all, it is a costly and time-consuming process, especially where large numbers are involved. The main reason given by the client for the assessment was the identification of strengths and weaknesses so that training programmes could be put in place. At a time when the training of financial advisers was a critical issue, this was not an unrealistic request from the client. The 'hidden agenda', however, was that the client also wanted to make quite a number of people redundant and would base their decisions on the results of the assessments. From my point of view, this changes the ball-game. It is one thing to sell assessment events for personal development reasons and quite another for redundancy purposes. The hidden agenda only came to light when the client asked how we might minimize disruptions, how we could prevent good sales people from leaving and how quickly we could implement the whole process without reducing morale. By probing their concerns behind these questions, we were able to gain the full picture.

In this example, my understanding of the client's needs had changed during the course of the discussions from purely assessment to assessment and redundancy. The client's main agenda was to select a consultancy on the basis of having handled this type of assignment before with minimum disruption, rather than on the quality of the assessments themselves.

This is a prime example of the importance of knowing your influencee's needs and wants. It puts you in a much better position to decide if you want to pursue matters further, or walk away. Case Histories 5.1 and 5.2 provide additional information on how power and influencing strategies are linked to understanding the influencee's needs.

3. Prepare your ground

Common sense dictates that before going into a negotiation you do your homework. There is nothing worse than going to a meeting, be it with a customer or a colleague, and trying to persuade and influence them with the wrong facts, the wrong agenda and the wrong tack. Good preparation provides you with additional ammunition to strengthen your case and, more importantly, gives you a tactical plan of how you can most effectively achieve your objectives. Having thought through issues and having the relevant information to hand means that decisions can be made there and then, even if only in principle. If you are trying to influence a potential client to buy your services or products, and they need clarification on product specifications or costs, your preparatory work means you will have the required information available. Through poor preparation many negotiations have to be reconvened, with the impetus – and your credibility – having being lost.

4. Involve the influencee(s)

The whole objective of persuading and influencing is to get the other person to do as you would like them to: it's about getting their *commitment and psychological 'buy-in'*. One of the most effective ways to secure commitment from the influencee is to involve them in the decision-making process. A joint decision enables the influencing and persuading process to be easier, often more innovative, and to gain momentum much quicker. If the influencee is involved in the negotiations and the decision-making process, they are demonstrating some commitment to it. As such, they will have some vested interest in ensuring the end result is successful. Usually, more innovative decisions are made through involving the influencee – the old adage that two heads are better than one.

5. Positively sell the benefits

Seeing things from the other person's point of view is an essential feature of effective influencing and persuading. The importance of selling the benefits is that you are matching the needs of the other person to what you are offering. Positively selling the benefits is about highlighting the match between their needs and your proposal and checking that their perceptions are similar to yours, eg:

*'You cited speed of response as an important criterion in deciding which orga-
nization to choose.... I hope I have sufficiently demonstrated the various assignments where we have achieved real results within timescales as short as yours.
From what I have said, do you have any reservations about our ability to
deliver quality work within tight timescales?'*

or

*Having jointly discussed the pros and cons of different options, do you feel we
have now reached a sensible outcome?.... I feel there are a number of other
benefits too in the decision we have reached, for example....*

Questioning, seeking clarification and gaining the input of the influencee are
important elements of positively selling benefits. This process allows you
insight into what the influencee is thinking and whether your views match the
other person's. (See Case History 5.3 for more information on how anticipating others' needs helps identify the most appropriate approach to selling the
benefits.)

6. Clinch objectives and then 'get out'

An important feature of influencing is knowing when you have achieved what
you set out to do and concluding the discussions. 'Quit while you're ahead' is
not a bad motto. This comes back to the earlier point made in Step 1 – that
negotiations have a knack of going full circle and in the process the goal-posts
usually move. In other words, if you achieve your main objectives quite early
on in a negotiation, you have to weigh up whether to quit with what you
have, or risk losing them as needs and circumstances change much later in the
meeting, rendering the earlier achievements obsolete. Obviously you have to
decide whether or not your objectives are interrelated or discrete. If the latter,
Step 6 definitely applies – clinch your objectives and quit. In short, when you
know you have influenced the other person on the benefits you have to offer,
you have achieved what you set out to do. The worst thing you could do is
keep introducing other benefits or features, one of which may not appeal to
the influencee, causing them to rethink their earlier decision.

7. Ensure prompt action is taken on decisions

Having spent time and energy on influencing others, a common, yet fatal,
mistake would be to think the hard work is done and to move on to something else. No doubt you have seen it with colleagues in a 'selling' situation,
where having put so much time into the influencing, they then slacken off on
the actual doing. Influencing someone in principle is second-best to influencing someone to take action – now. Indeed, the process of influencing and
persuading can be seen as a two-stage process. The first is where you convince
the individual at an intellectual and emotional level that your recommendations are worth pursuing. The second element is converting 'I agree, it's a
good idea and it meets my requirements', into affirmative action. If speed of

service or delivery was important in the client's decision-making process, the worst thing you could do, having persuaded them to use you, is not to take prompt action. You need to demonstrate that you practise what you preach.

THE KEY PRINCIPLES OF INFLUENCING AND PERSUADING OTHERS

This section focuses not so much on the work of any one psychologist or academic, but on the key principles of influencing and persuading others.

- retribution
- reciprocity, and
- reason.

The three Rs, as they are sometimes described, are the main strategies used by managers to gain commitment. Let's look at these three Rs in more detail.

Retribution strategies

As the name suggests, these are strategies which rely on both overt and covert threats to win the other person's compliance. The whole tone of this style is based on coercion and intimidation. Retribution includes straightforward threats, eg:

If you do not do this for me, you'll regret it or I will make life difficult for you,

to the less blatant use of social pressure, eg:

Everyone else agrees this is the way we ought to go, what about you?

Reciprocity strategies

These strategies are reliant on compliance being achieved, through mutual or one-sided benefit. Let's look first at the mutual benefit approach, which is based on a 'win-win' strategy, eg:

You will benefit by this through ... while I gain because ...

to a more 'win-lose' strategy of:

You know how important this is to me; if you will do X for me, I will reciprocate in the future.

Reason strategies

These are based on *facts* and knowing the 'leverages' which will influence the other person. As with the other influencing strategies, both 'push' and 'pull' approaches exist. A 'pull' approach might be something along the lines of:

Well Tina, it is important you make up your own mind. You know what my own position is. Here are all the facts and figures I have available; let me know what you think, after you have had a chance to digest the information

while the 'push' approach would go something like:

Tina, the figures prove that we have to do X; it's there in black and white.

It is important to appreciate, however, that reasoning approaches to influencing others are not reliant on dispassionate logic, where the other person is swayed by facts and figures. Reasoning can and does entail shaping a case to appeal to the other person's needs. This is what meant by knowing the 'leverages' by which to influence the other person. If I knew, for example, that the person I was trying to influence was cost-conscious, the lever I might use would be:

and of course, this particular approach also has the benefit of being highly cost-effective and, I'm sure you'll agree, that is an important consideration in these difficult times

provided, of course, that this genuinely was the case!

Case History 5.1

How Many Types of Influencing Strategies Can You Come up With?

A number of influencing strategies can be used to persuade others, but the ability to influence and persuade is strongly determined by: *credibility* and *power*. You have to have the respect of others if you are to truly influence them. Whether it is influencing customers, colleagues, or an entire organization (ie, in the case of a chief executive influencing the organization to adopt his/her new vision), without personal credibility the process will be an up-hill struggle. Credibility rests fundamentally on the actions and behaviour of the individual. Power, too, is important, because that rests predominantly on the authority of the individual. A shop-floor worker, for example, may have credibility through their know-how and technical skills, but if they do not have the power, they are unlikely to be able to influence others by credibility alone. This last point highlights why power in its broadest sense is an important feature of empowerment.

Coming back then to influencing strategies, the main distinction is between *push* and *pull* strategies. Push strategies are those which rely on the individual being personally involved in getting people to change their minds or perspectives. The advantage of this approach is that it can generate quick results, because the manager is on hand to personally push others to change. The downside is that as soon as the manager is not on the scene, the momentum for change diminishes and people are more likely to revert to their old way of doing things. Pull strategies, on the other hand, rely on presenting a case so persuasively that others are drawn to it. The benefit of this approach is that change is likely to be enduring, as it relies on the individuals' own volition. The downside is that it does take much longer. In tactical terms these two strategies can be described as *'offensive'* (I make up your mind for you) and *'defensive'* (You can make up your own mind). Within these two terms there are a number of variations. The tactics within pushing strategies are:

force: 'I'm telling you, your only option is ... '
assertion: 'I would like you to seriously consider ...'
rules and standards: 'the health and safety regulations require you to ...'
exchange: 'if you do X for me, I will do Y for you ...'.

The tactics within pulling strategies are:

personal magnetism: people do things because of your charisma
visioning: people do things because of the vision you have painted
environmental management: people do things because of the culture you have created
Joint problem-solving: people want to do things because it was a joint decision-making process.

Case History 5.2

Power and Influencing: Know your Power Type

Management and leadership can be described as the *process* of influencing the activities of others. Power can be described as the *influence potential* of the manager or as the resource which enables a manager to influence others. There are seven sources of power, which can be described as follows:

Authoritarian power: this is based on fear. A manager using authoritarian power is able to influence because others fear that non-compliance will lead to punishment, such as undesirable work assignments, reprimands or dismissals.
Connection power: is based on the manager's 'connections' with influential or important persons, either inside or outside the organization. A manager using connection power is able to influence because others want the favour or to avoid the disfavour of the powerful connection.

Knowledge power: is based on the individual's possession of expertise, skill and knowledge which gain the respect of others. Their knowledge gives the individual credibility in influencing the work behaviour of others.

Information power: is based on an individual's possession of or access to information that is perceived as valuable to others. This power-base influences others because they need this information or want to be 'in on things'.

Status power: is based on the position held by the individual. The higher the status, the higher the legitimate power tends to be. A manager high on status power influences others because they feel that this person has the right by virtue of position in the organization to expect that suggestions be followed.

Personal power: is based on the individual's personality traits. An individual scoring high in personal power is generally liked and admired by others because of personality. The liking for and identification with an individual influences others.

Reward power: is based on an individual's ability to provide rewards for other people. By providing rewards they are able to gain others' compliance.

Case History 5.3

Situational Influencing Techniques: A Day in the Life of a Manager

The aim of this section is to highlight how, during a typical day, a manager will use different influencing strategies depending on the situations he or she finds themself in.

Pam, a business analyst employed by a leading food producer, had an 8.00 am meeting booked with the regional sales managers. The main agenda was to discuss the downward trend in brand-label products and the surge in own-label products in supermarkets. The independent figures gathered from their main suppliers were clear: in the past six months alone, the shift towards own-label products had been quite considerable. Pam was firmly of the view that the business should produce both branded and own-label products and take advantage of what she saw as being an emerging trend in the market place. She knew this move was likely to be dismissed by the regional managers, given the market dominance of their own brand and the nervousness about moving to less expensive own-label brands, not least because of the knock-on effect this would have on their bonuses.

Pam had a fairly good idea of how the sales managers would respond to her recommendations, so she decided that her best chance of influencing them would be through 'guiding' them to her preferred decision, rather than telling them what to do. As they were independent types who felt they knew their business better than she did (claiming they were closer to the customers), she knew they would resist being told what to do. Influencing in this case was based on the '*pull*' strategy of having a clear idea of what she wanted to achieve and using *persuasion* and *joint problem-solving* to achieve her objectives.

Later that day she was required to provide the divisional board with an update on the business and her short- to medium-term plans. Again, she knew that she would be challenged on a number of points, unless she had the facts and business case to back her up. One of the pieces of work she knew would be influential was some benchmarking work which had been published by a leading consultancy's food and drink division. The benchmark work highlighted that not only did their main competitors get a small but growing amount of their business from own-label products, but that this was likely to be a rapidly expanding market, given the demand for greater choice by customers. She also had her own figures which showed that the own-label brand would be highly profitable, given the large volumes involved and special 'bulk' packages the stores were likely to sell. Bringing in an external consultant (*knowledge power*) would probably carry more weight with the divisional board than her own recommendations.

Her third meeting that day was with the company's main wholesalers, who act as the 'middle-men' between themselves and the smaller retailers. Her main concern was that their best-selling product was not getting the shelf-space it warranted in the wholesalers' warehouses. With the company's products being less visible, the small shop-keepers were not loading them onto their trolley. Pam knew full well that the wholesalers could not afford to lose their business, given they were the leading confectioners in the UK market. Her *coercive* tactic of, 'We expect a 10% increase in the sale of product X, through better positioning and advertising within the next two months, or we get close to another wholesaler', was not a usual tactic, but one she felt would get quick results.

KEY ACTION AND LEARNING POINTS

1. What have been the key learning points for you in this chapter?

2. What are the main actions you need to take to improve your influencing and persuading style; what are the timescales and specific objectives?

3. What are the main obstacles to you achieving your main objectives. What do you need to do to overcome them?

Learning points from the case histories

The main points to emerge from the Case Histories are that influencing and persuasion are strongly connected with power and personal credibility – a point captured by the opening quote: 'Influential people have power, but not all powerful people have influence'. Case History 5.1, for example, demonstrates how 'push' and 'pull' strategies can be used, each with their strengths and limitations. Case History 5.2 describes in more detail how individuals can have different sources of power and how some sources of power are very specific in nature: knowledge and information power; while others are more far-reaching: personal and status power. Finally, Case History 5.3 demonstrates how influencing strategies are situationally based. While expert power might be most suited to situation X, status power might be more appropriate in situation Y.

SUMMARY

The business case

The ability to influence and persuade is a critical managerial skill. Taking a macro business perspective, the influencing of three main audiences is deemed highly important: the City, customers and employees. Influencing and persuading is important simply because *all* business interactions are so reliant on it. Marketing, advertising and individual face-to-face meetings all rely on influencing and persuading others. An ability to influence effectively provides organizations with a competitive advantage.

Putting it into practice

This chapter highlights seven practical steps to effectively influence and persuade others. The essence of these seven steps is to make influencing a two-way process, which matches 'needs' with 'benefits'. Effective influencing is achieved through clarifying what your objectives are, having prepared your ground and completed your homework. If at all possible, the influencee should be involved in the negotiations – this not only gets their commitment to a successful outcome but invariably results in more creative solutions.

The key principles

The key principles of influencing and persuading fit into three main categories: retribution, reciprocity and reason. Each of these strategies uses different approaches to gain commitment based on factual evidence (reason), to 'win-lose' (retribution) and 'win-win' (reciprocity) tactics. Understanding others' influencing strategies enables you to better appreciate 'where they are all coming from' and how best to respond.

Section 3

ACHIEVING RESULTS

Chapter 6

MANAGING PERFORMANCE

What you measure is what you get
(Kaplan and Norton, 1992)

WHAT YOU CAN EXPECT

After reading this chapter, you will have a better understanding of:

- the key principles of managing performance

- how you can improve your skills in managing others' performance

- new initiatives in managing performance

- how the performance management process links in with other organizational processes

- some of the pitfalls in managing performance

- the role of managing performance in managing change

- how leading organizations manage performance

———— OVER TO YOU ————

1. What are the key issues you have regarding the way performance is managed in your organization?

2. What then are the key points you would like to learn from this chapter?

3. How do you think the way performance is currently managed needs changing?

4. Does your organization place greater importance on future performance or past performance?

THE BUSINESS CASE

Managing performance is critical at the organizational and individual level. At the organizational level, the issues are: what are the key results the business *needs to achieve* and how will the business know if they *are being achieved*? At the individual level, the issues are: how can individuals most *effectively achieve* the business objectives and how will individuals and the business know if they *are being achieved*? Managing performance effectively, therefore, has several implications:

▪ *Individual* and organizational objectives are closely linked.

▪ *Mechanisms* need to be in place which enable individuals and managers to monitor their performance.

▪ *Managing* performance is a continuous process, which happens in 'the now', rather than being a process which is based on reviewing how things have been performed.

▪ *Individuals* and their managers alike have responsibility for monitoring their own performance.

▪ *The focus* is clearly on achieving results and outcomes rather than on job descriptions and limiting responsibilities.

Managing performance should be a 'living' and proactive process which exists to ensure that both organizational and individual objectives are achieved. If performance is managed effectively there should be *no reason why all individuals and all business units do not achieve their targets*. This may sound idealistic, but it is possible, through consistently monitoring performance and responding to the feedback being received. Let's compare managing a business with piloting an aeroplane: both have complex information systems; both have to take into account external events and adapt to them. In the case of the business it is the fluctuation of currency rates; responding to what competitors might be doing; and responding to the changing needs of customers. This is not dissimilar to the pilot who would be monitoring wind direction, speed, turbulence and the flight path of other planes. The effectiveness with which a business is managed, therefore depends on:

▪ *getting* accurate and regular feedback on performance and

▪ *responding* effectively to that information.

The final part of the equation is to have a human resource system loosely aligned with business indicators to ensure that people are being rewarded for delivering results, in the most effective way. Both *what* is achieved and *how* it is achieved need to be an integral part of the human resource system.

The bottom line is that managing performance is a powerful means by which an organization can achieve tangible business results. Effective organizations have an integrated process, which links business performance to individual performance which in turn is linked to pay, training and career management.

PUTTING IT INTO PRACTICE

As a manager, what practical steps do you need to take to effectively manage performance? This section explores the following themes:

1. Putting performance processes in place.
2. Gaining employee buy-in.
3. Conducting performance management meetings.
4. Managing the ongoing process.

Putting performance processes in place

For a manager to provide meaningful feedback to others, he/she needs to have performance processes in place. At the business level, some of the areas which might be measured are: levels of customer satisfaction; costs; wastage; complaints by customers; cash flow; market share; key quality indicators, etc. Different individuals and project teams will have responsibilities for different performance areas and it is important a manager has detailed information on these. Holding people accountable without a clear definition of their objectives and without a performance process in place would be extremely difficult. If, for example, levels of customer satisfaction are poor, then different teams will need to take very specific corrective actions. Once it has been identified what the nature of the corrective actions might be, it is important that timescales are defined, along with outcomes. In other words, it is not enough to say, 'We will reduce the number of customer complaints' – as such a loose definition is difficult to quantify and measure. A more precise definition might be, 'To reduce customer complaints relating to quality of advice by 80% and relating to keeping delivery dates by 70%. Both these goals to be achieved within six months (November 30)'. Both paper records and management information systems should then be in place to ensure that these goals are being tracked on a daily, weekly or monthly basis – whatever is appropriate for your situation.

2. Gaining employee buy-in

The main problem employees have with traditional performance management systems is that objectives are presented to them, with little or no room for negotiation. Their manager's defence is that their objectives in turn were given to them, or they were not aware that objectives could be negotiated. If, as has been argued, the main purpose of managing performance should be to improve performance and be future-oriented, then the involvement of subordinates is critical. A joint discussion is an extremely productive way of getting commitment to achieving objectives for the following reasons: the subordinate feels a sense of ownership in what has been agreed; they have had a chance to discuss what factors are likely to impede on help them in their cause; they can agree timescales and clarify the final outcome. This process is not a tick-box exercise, but is based on the view that the job-holder knows their job better

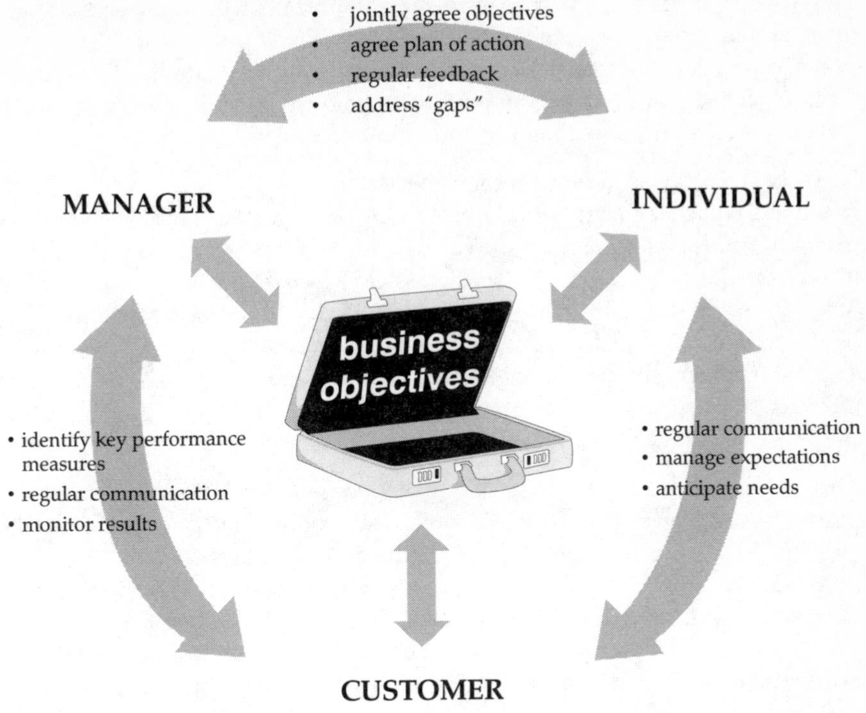

- jointly agree objectives
- agree plan of action
- regular feedback
- address "gaps"

MANAGER

INDIVIDUAL

business objectives

- identify key performance measures
- regular communication
- monitor results

- regular communication
- manage expectations
- anticipate needs

CUSTOMER

Figure 6.1 *Achieving business objectives through managing performance*

than any one else and consequently is the best person to be involved in discussing how business objectives can be achieved most effectively.

3. Conducting performance management meetings

Having raised the importance of employee involvement in the negotiation of performance improvement, what about the interview itself? The key steps can be referred to as the five Is:

Information on business requirements:
This is the opportunity for manager and subordinate to review how the business is performing and what the future holds. This provides a meaningful background against which personal objectives can be discussed and reviewed. It is also extremely useful in providing the individual with the bigger picture, namely, how their own objectives fit into the overall scale of things, and how their role and objectives relate to other departments.

Involve in open discussion:
Once the business scene has been set and the broad objectives for the coming year have been mentioned, both manager and subordinate then need to openly discuss the 'what' and the 'how'. Clarifying the 'what' means discussing objec-

tives so that manager and individual are in agreement on the outcome, the timescales and resources which will be needed. The 'how' focuses the discussion on the plan of action which the individual will need to adopt to achieve those objectives. This stage is important to gain the individual's commitment and enthusiasm, through a joint negotiation process.

Identify strengths and development needs:
It is important that the manager discusses his/her perception of the candidate's strengths and development needs, so that the implications of how this might impact on their objectives can be discussed. By clarifying what the subordinate's strengths are, the discussion can usefully move on to how these might be capitalized on. Equally, development needs and how to meet them can be discussed, which should then involve coaching and mentoring by the line manager.

Improvement criteria:
This stage entails summarizing the main conclusions of the meeting and setting future plans: the objectives which have been jointly agreed; how the individual can capitalize on their strengths and what development interventions need to be in place. The focus on improvement criteria actively addresses how future performance can be improved. Issues for discussion might be how the working relationship between the boss and subordinate could be improved, or what performance feedback from customers and colleagues needs to be acted on.

Incentivize:
Motivation and incentives are important elements of any performance dialogue. During this phase of the discussions, not only do pay and performance-related bonuses need to be considered, but also factors such as career and psychological aspirations. The career aspirations focus on the type of role the individual would like to be doing in the short and longer term; while the psychological aspirations help the manager appreciate what the individual's main motivations are. For some individuals job satisfaction might be gained from regularly experiencing different parts of the business, while for others it might be gaining more in-depth specialist expertise.

4. Managing the ongoing process

For performance to improve, you as a manager need to have systems in place which provide ongoing business-related information. These systems might include informal and formal progress checks, software packages which 'map' personal performance with business performance, and asking reportees to keep a record of their own progress on performance. Self-directed performance management is important in flatter organizational structures, where individuals have greater responsibility for managing themselves.

THE KEY PRINCIPLES OF MANAGING PERFORMANCE

For some managers, managing performance is a paper and pencil exercise, which culminates in the year-end performance appraisal. Unfortunately, this model dramatically limits the benefits to the organization. The reality is that if used effectively, managing performance can be a very powerful business tool enabling both the business and individuals to benefit. So what are the key principles enabling this to happen?

Managing performance vs performance management

An important principle of managing performance is getting the best from others. The focus then, is on improving performance, on achieving results efficiently and effectively. This proactive stance is far more constructive and dynamic than a process which seeks to ensure that people know what is expected of them and then measures how they have performed at the end of a set period. *Performance management* is often closely associated with this latter view, namely that it is a process which is administered – not actively managed. *Managing performance*, on the other hand, relies strongly on the emotional energy and commitment of a manager to improve performance, through encouraging, praising and rewarding others. The ethos behind managing performance is to provide subordinates with on-going feedback from which they can learn, enabling them to monitor their own performance and check that their actions are producing beneficial outcomes. In short, managing performance is about constantly making sure that desired outcomes are being achieved and focusing on performance improvement, while performance management is usually associated with processes, such as objective-setting and appraisal reviews which focus on past behaviours.

Enabling vs monitoring

Those managers who manage performance well do so by making it easy for individuals to perform their roles to the best of their abilities. They enable through providing regular feedback on performance, removing barriers which impede performance and providing others with learning opportunities. This is in sharp contrast to a performance management process which *monitors* performance, rather than actively managing it. This latter approach can bring about 'blame-cultures', where individuals are penalized and chastised for past mistakes and events. Years of this debilitating blame culture have led many organizations to rethink the purpose of their performance management systems – Case History 6.1 provides further information on this.

On-going vs static

Managing performance should be an ongoing process, rather than an annual or bi-annual affair. While there need to be more formal reviews of performance, these should be an adjunct to the process which goes on daily. An on-going process immediately reinforces effective performance and provides feed-back on poor performance – the essence of performance improvement. Unfortunately, for many organizations it is a static process, which has a very narrow remit. This static element is further endorsed by the process of *rating performance*. A numerical rating scale can and often does reduce managing performance to an exercise where both the boss and subordinate feel they are getting very little from it, encouraging a 'pass/fail' mentality. The on-going process of managing performance is far more interactive, relying heavily on the skill of the manager to provide constructive feedback. An ongoing process is only possible if the manager is able to regularly access information on business performance. After all, it is difficult to provide meaningful feedback to others if there are no tangible data on which to base the feedback.

Case History 6.1

Why so many Performance Management Systems Fail: The Case of Halcyon Electricity

'I'm afraid it is that time of the year again, where I am having to chase managers for their performance appraisal forms ... we've put up with it for so long, that we need a major overhaul; tinkering at the edges just won't do'. These were the words of the personnel manager working in the post-privatization electricity industry, where internal project teams were working to evaluate how systems and processes needed to change to 'add-value' to the business. So why had it taken Halcyon so long to take action and why did they want to change it now? The answer to the first part is fairly straightforward – Halcyon did not feel compelled to change, it had a perfor-mance system it was happy with; it met its short and longer term require-ments and was 'part of the furniture'. Perhaps it is not surprising that Halcyon did not feel the need to change on several accounts: first, in a fairly stable business environment (the demand for electricity is fairly consistent), the company was able to plan its succession planning perfectly adequately through the performance appraisal process. Second, the culture of the busi-ness was not one of 'accountability' but of 'paternalism'. The business provided job security in return for 'a fair day's work'; employees were not expected or required to demonstrate what value they were adding to the business. Halcyon was probably no different from the other public utility companies which offered their employees a 'job for life' and where the aver-age length of service was around 15 years.

The reason Halcyon wanted to change the performance management system now was because it just did not fit into the business-driven culture they were striving to create. The system was seen as bureaucratic, time-intensive and exacerbating poor morale and performance. Many managers had received insufficient training in handling issues of poor performance, preferring instead to let them go unnoticed 'for a quiet life'. The appraisal system relied heavily on the ratings given to subordinates, which were hotly contested by the individual, given that so much depended on them – pay, promotion prospects, etc. There was disagreement over how consistent and fair these ratings were – some managers viewed the whole process as a paper and pencil exercise and treated it with contempt, while others saw that it had some value and would accordingly spend time with subordinates to provide them with detailed and meaningful feedback.

In short, the reason why Halcyon and other organizations like it were not getting added value from their performance management systems was ostensibly to do with the *'ethos'* and *process* behind it. The ethos was one of appraising people's performance once a year. This was a chance for managers to either 'hit subordinates with a stick', or to make the process so bland that the manager, the reportee and the organization got little of value from it. The actual process of having a once-yearly review which was largely dependent on a tick-box process did not help matters either. Events which happened six months ago, for example, were not reviewed with any real accuracy and the very act of reviewing performance lent itself to blaming others. This was often compounded by the reportee's defensiveness that anything they said on personal development needs would be 'written down and held as evidence against them' – resulting in a poor performance rating.

A Personal View 6.2

How Can Managing Performance be made More Effective?

This section builds on many of the ideas already mentioned in the chapter and evaluates what can be done *practically* to manage performance more effectively. The paradigm shift is from one where performance management is used primarily for administrative reasons, which benefit the organization (ie, for succession planning, identification of training needs, an opportunity to pass on objectives) to one which is more oriented to the needs of the business and the individual alike. How might this work in practice?

Let's take a specific point in case: the need for an organization to have managers who are strongly customer-oriented, so that the organization gets more repeat business and can differentiate itself from its competitors through its quality of service. In this context, it is important that managers receive regular feedback on how they are performing against a set of 'customer-oriented criteria'. Being customer-oriented is less to do with a set of processes (getting products out on time and within cost) and more to do with behaviours: listening to customers, better understanding their needs and requirements, working in partnership with them. How then can a performance management process assess and provide feedback on behaviours? The starting point would be an open discussion between a manager and reportee on what objectives they have and how they can most effectively be achieved. This discussion should focus on the behaviours which the reportee would need to demonstrate to achieve successful outcomes. Having established critical behaviours for successful outcomes, these could be *integrated* through all-round feedback into a performance management process. This form of feedback is reliant on subordinates, colleagues and managers (hence the all-round perspective) providing their views on how the individual actually matches up to the critical behaviours. This information is then fed back to the candidate, providing immediate information on how internal customers perceive the individual's effectiveness across a range of areas. This on-going feedback enables an individual to *actively manage their own performance,* knowing quite accurately how they are performing through the feedback of others.

This reliance on constructive feedback against a set of core behaviours can be a very powerful way of creating a performance culture, for it firmly places accountability in the hands of the individual. In other words, the most effective way of changing your appraisal feedback is to change your actual behaviour. This type of approach can also be a very powerful way of introducing new values and business needs. If, as in the life assurance industry, quality of service and advice has been a major issue, this can be quickly monitored and addressed through the all-round feedback process, which can be conducted weekly, monthly or at any time intervals which are useful to the individual.

KEY ACTION AND LEARNING POINTS

1. What have been the main learning points for you in this chapter?

2. What are the key changes you would like to make; what are the timescales and what are the main barriers you need to overcome?

3. How responsive would the people you manage be to continuous improvement and having regular feedback on performance from peers, colleagues and customers?

Learning points from the case histories

The case history and the personal view highlight how performance management and managing performance are dramatically different in their approaches. In the case of Halcyon Electricity, the 'traditional' performance management system had been part of the furniture. Managers ritualistically completed the performance appraisal forms, but saw it as a laborious chore from which they and their subordinates gained little value. Potentially the system was very divisive, with colleagues comparing and judging the fairness of the system of their rating relative to others. The continuous managing performance approach, however, provides regular feedback on performance to individuals. It is a process which constantly monitors where the organization needs to be, with where it is now. This type of information enables necessary interventions to be made quickly and as the need arises, so that successful outcomes can be achieved.

SUMMARY

The business case

Managing performance is a way for organizations to *differentiate* themselves from the competition and dramatically *improve* the performance of the business. Organizations which are highly effective in this area *integrate* key business drivers into the performance objectives of employees. Both business and individual performance are reviewed on a *regular* basis – which for fast moving consumer goods companies might actually be on a daily basis. *Continuously* managing performance enables organizations to capitalize on and reward what is being done well and act quickly on things which are not producing the desired outcomes – rather than taking corrective action once mistakes have been made.

Putting it into practice

Putting effective management of performance into practice requires a number of things to be in place. First, there is a need for information systems which keep track of business and individual performance. The value of the system depends on what information 'goes in' and how this information is used, and today's Windows-based software, with its 'user-friendly' system should help. Once it has been agreed how business objectives need to be integrated with individuals' objectives, manager and subordinate need to negotiate. The negotiation needs to be a genuine two-way process where gaining the commitment of the individual is a critical objective. The manager and individual need to discuss *what* will be achieved and *how* it will happen.

The key principles

The principles underlying the managing performance process being suggested here are important if it is going to be radically different from many of the more 'traditional' approaches. The key principles are: the process needs to be a continuous one relying on regular feedback against key criteria; the manager's role is to ensure individuals are encouraged to learn from their experiences and to improve their own performance as they go along, rather than a role which only monitors and reviews performance. The forward-looking element is critical to its success.

Chapter 7

MANAGING CHANGE

An intelligent company integrates 'what's going on out there' with 'how we do things around here'
(Haeckel and Nolan, 1993)

WHAT YOU CAN EXPECT

After reading this chapter, you will have a better understanding of:

- the practical aspects of managing change

- what the difficulties of change are

- how to overcome potential barriers to change

- the psychological costs of change

- how most effectively to introduce change

- the organizational issues surrounding change

- the different stages of a change programme

OVER TO YOU

1. What are the key business drivers behind the need for change in your organization?

2. What are your objectives, the timescales you are working to and the resources you will need?

3. How will you know when the change programme is completed or if it is successful? In other words, describe as fully as possible how the end result of change should look and feel.

4. At which stage of the change cycle are you; what therefore are the most pressing needs and what are some of the lessons you can learn from previous change programmes?

5. What does your organization do well, which should be incorporated into the new culture/environment you are trying to create?

THE BUSINESS CASE

The one *certainty* in business is change. Those organizations which are change-oriented – looking for better, more efficient ways of doing things – are those which are most likely to gain a competitive edge. Successful organizations anticipate changes in the market place or in the needs of customers and gear themselves to respond; they appreciate that change is not a 'stop-start' process, but an on-going quest to sustain competitive advantage. *Managing change* is the active process of coordinating 'how we do things around here' with most effectively meeting 'what's going on out there'. Managing change usually entails all or some of the following.

Systems

This usually entails changes in technology or products. The 'hard' changes can either be enhancements to an existing product or the development of completely new systems. Change in this sense is ensuring that the right technology, systems and machinery are in place to meet the needs of customers. Banks are currently at the forefront of systems-led changes. The introduction of computer technology is dramatically changing the way banks operate – 24-hour telephone banking, cash-machines which provide up-to-date information on your account and the introduction of 'smart cards' mean that a customer need never enter a high street branch.

Processes

This entails changing business processes, ranging from the way a car insurance company processes your claim form to a complete rethink in the way an organization meets the needs of its customers. For example, business process re-engineering looks at the processes involved in getting products or services to end-users and how value can be added at every stage. By aligning internal processes with the needs of customers, *dramatic* improvements in efficiency can be brought about. Changing processes entails both people and technology and has been forced upon many organizations by competitors cutting lead times in the introduction of new products, building to a higher specification and often at lower cost. The end result is that many organizations are moving to project-based multi-skilled teams, which are responsible for managing themselves and having far greater contact with customers than before. The emphasis is on a process which 'uncomplicates' internal 'boundaries' so that products and services are efficiently and effectively delivered to customers.

People

This can mean anything from changing the 'hearts and minds' of people to providing technical training to ensure changes in systems can be managed by their operators. It is arguably people who are critical to the ultimate success of a company, rather than systems or processes themselves. While systems and process improvements can bring about incremental change, it is the harnessing of well-trained, motivated and empowered people which brings about sustained improvement. While processes and technology can soon become out of date, people who are geared to change and work on continuously developing themselves are able to constantly 'renew' products, processes and services as a natural evolutionary process. *The bottom line is that a competitive advantage is gained by organizations which are geared to continuous improvement.*

PUTTING IT INTO PRACTICE

As a manager, what are the things *you* need to be doing to effectively manage and introduce change? You may find the model in Figure 7.1, which is based on the work of Professor Trybus, useful. Let's look at the various components in further detail.

$$EC = A \times B \times C > Z$$

EC = Energy and enthusiasm for change

A = Dissatisfaction with the present

B = Attractiveness of the benefits of change

C = Clarity and simplicity of transition

Z = Psychological and economic costs of change

Figure 7.1 *Gaining commitment for change*

STEP 1: PREPARING FOR CHANGE

A = Dissatisfaction with the present

Perhaps it is stating the obvious, but you will never get *enthusiasm* for change if people can not see why they have to change. Moving people out of their 'comfort zone' is not an easy task at the best of times and needs to be carefully managed. To try and do so without selling change is causing unnecessary hard work for yourself. An important element of selling the need for change is to encourage subordinates to take ownership and be actively involved in the decision-making process. The need for change becomes more obvious if colleagues and subordinates have the right information and are able to openly discuss the implications and ramifications of different scenarios. People have to be dissatisfied with the present before they will seriously think about change.

So, how do you actually overcome comments such as, 'if it ain't broke don't fix it'? As a manager it may be necessary to make people feel uncomfortable to get them out of their 'comfort zone'; or it may be necessary to provide people with information so they can see that things could be made more effective, even though they may be acceptable as they are. It is only by broadening people's horizons and expectations that the attitude of 'I don't see why we need to change' can be addressed. By providing opportunities which enable people to *see*, the need for change becomes more compelling.

Case History 7.1 describes how involving employees in defining a change programme is not difficult or costly and yet dramatically increases its success rate.

B = The benefits of change

You may have convinced others that the department and the organization needs to change its working practices, but unless you respond to the 'what's in it for me?' question, you will not get the enthusiasm and commitment you need to create the momentum for change. Understandably, for many people change is threatening and uncomfortable, because they are stepping into the unknown. As a manager, however, there is a lot you can do to minimize this resistance to change. Creating the vision of the future is often not enough, unless you personalize it for individuals, by showing what this will actually mean for them. Many managers start to sell the benefit of change by identifying the frustrations employees experience, such as repetitive work which lacks stimulation, little or no team work, and little opportunity to exercise judgement. By using these as 'leverages' in *selling* the benefits of change, a manager will not have his/her message falling on deaf ears. After all, who would resist change if they will benefit from it? The answer is, those who feel they do not have the skills, expertise or know-how to perform in this new environment. This then leads on to the next point.

C = The ease of transition

For individuals to embrace change *enthusiastically*, they need to know what is required of them, have a clear idea of the timescales they are working to and of the expected outcome. You are after all asking them to embark on a journey and unless you specify what the destination is, how long the journey will take and the means of getting from A to B, you are creating unnecessary unease and discomfort. It is important to be realistic with people at this stage, in highlighting the likely difficulties and challenges that will result from the change programme. Psychological preparation of individuals is just as important as the more tangible factors. By knowing what to expect and having the tools to deal with these eventualities, individuals are more likely to feel in control of change.

Many organizations find that development centres or training workshops are very beneficial in 'scenario modelling' and create the situations which individuals will have to face in the change process. Case History 7.2 describes this in more detail.

Z = The psychological and economic costs of change

Unless you create and manage the situation, so that stages A, B and C are fully articulated, the *commitment* you generate for change will be muted. It is worth appreciating how threatening people can find change, especially if they feel they are not in control of a situation. Changing people's negative perceptions is important if the psychological barriers are to be overcome. The more effective manager will present change as an opportunity for personal growth and development; will create an environment where people know if they make a mistake they will not be humiliated; and will provide individuals with personal coaching and development so that they are more equipped to deal with change. Regular feedback on performance and celebrating successes are all means by which a manager can overcome the negative perceptions associated with change.

Finally, change needs to have a 'pay-back' to the business. Unless the financial benefits of change are attractive and sustainable, the business case for a major change programme cannot be supported.

STEP 2: MANAGING THE TRANSITION

Once the case for change has been prepared, it has to be converted into *action*. In many change programmes there is a transitionary stage, which has to be managed carefully: the momentum for change can be boosted or falter; hearts can be won or lost, because it is not too late to go back to the old way of doing things – the point of no return has not yet been reached. A sequence of stages which enables new behaviour to be successfully embedded is shown in Figure 7.2.

The manager first needs to create *awareness* of what the company/department is trying to achieve. Unless the objective is articulated in the form of goals and targets, the 'hearts and minds' of individuals are difficult to capture. Awareness of objectives and the need for the change programme only become embedded through regular communication, feedback and up-dates on perfor-

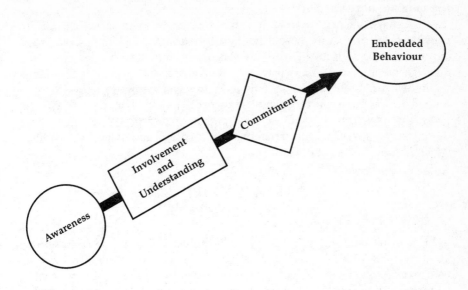

Figure 7.2 *Managing the transition*

mance. Creating awareness of what the organization is trying to achieve also comes about by getting people *involved* and thinking about how the new environment will look and feel so that they have some specific image of what they should be aiming for. This then leads on to the second process, which is getting the *involvement and understanding* of people you want to take along with you on your change journey. Involvement is a critical part of any change process, because individuals are much more likely to undertake something which they feel they have a say in and some control over. Involvement should be real, rather than token. Some of the most effective change programmes devolve key decisions to action groups and project teams, who are given parameters of responsibility, encouraged to make firm recommendations and see those through to implementation. Involvement leads to a better insight into and understanding of a situation. This understanding provides meaning and clarity in the need for change.

If you want a successful change programme, ensure that you get some early success; as the saying goes, begin to eat the elephant with small bite-size pieces. Nothing engenders confidence and *commitment* better than success, so ensure that what you are asking people to do is realistic within the timescales you are working to, is clearly measurable and has a specific outcome. With these factors in mind, you and your team will recognize success when you achieve it. This sounds rather elementary, but it is surprising how often it is overlooked in major change programmes. Case History 7.3 highlights the problems fear of change can create. Celebrating early successes is one way of reducing the impact of fear.

What most change programmes aim for is to bring about change in people's *behaviour*: from the old to the new way of doing things. Whether change is being introduced to provide better customer service, an improvement in quality standards, whatever – the bottom-line is that it invariably requires a change in behaviour. It is in getting individuals to relearn behaviours which are more in tune with the company's desired culture and change plans, that many programmes experience greatest difficulty. The longer-term objectives of any change programme are to bring about new behaviours, which become second nature.

THE KEY PRINCIPLES OF MANAGING CHANGE

Change management is an enormous subject area and to try to cover all the key principles would require a whole book in its own right. This section focuses on Kurt Lewin's influential work, which identifies three distinct phases which both individuals and organizations go through, to bring about lasting change. These three phases are shown in Figure 7.3.

Figure 7.3 *Lewin's model of change*

Unfreezing

For change to take place, people need to accept that things are currently not right and have a genuine desire to change. This stage is characterized by *identifying* what needs to be changed and the reasons behind the change. It should also entail analysis of what the organization currently does well, so that this can be incorporated in the new way of doing things. Many change programmes end up by having 'thrown the baby out with the bath water'; ie, the need for change is so frenetic that the positive aspects of how the organization functions are not considered when reshaping the future. It is important to begin change from a position of strength – this organization does a lot of things well, as well as needing to do many other things better.

Changing

This is the implementation of the new through the development of new *attitudes* and *behaviour*. This stage is characterized by planning and coordinating the new business processes, and where the momentum for change is at its greatest, where emotions and feelings are heightened, where uncertainty and flux seems to be the order of the day. It is at this stage that there are psychological, social and physical consequences of change. The psychological and social issues arise from people being unsure what the future holds, rumours abound, and the grapevine system is rife with speculation. People try to seek reassurance and try to understand change within their own model of the world. Ultimately people are seeking a 'comfort zone' or haven, where they can make order out of apparent disorder. This is where a major obstacle to change can occur, where what the organization is trying to do is not understood by the people whom it will impact. Organizations going through reengineering projects can experience difficulty gaining 'buy-in' from employees because their traditional model of who they are and what they do has been reshaped. They are often asked to work with loose job descriptions, in multi-disciplined project teams and with much greater autonomy, all of which is likely to be contrary to what they're used to.

Refreezing

This stage entails *consolidating* the new environment through reinforcement and supporting mechanisms. It is characterized by greater stability and less frenetic energy. It is a chance for people to review what has been achieved and assess what else needs to be done. The refreezing stage, while by no means the end of the change process, does signal that most of the major changes are in place. Performance appraisal systems and the way people are recruited and rewarded are often linked to the new way of doing things. For example, if change is necessitated by the need to offer customers a better quality of service, this is often a key issue on which people are appraised and rewarded. Often 'new blood' is brought into the organization to provide a fresh injection of ideas and confirmation that the old ways of doing things are gone.

Case History 7.1

Selling the Need for Change through Involvement

Imagine the following scenario: you are the manager of a division of a highly successful household pharmaceutical company, ABC plc, producing medical gauzes, bandages and cotton wool. The raw ingredient is imported from India and manufactured in the north of England at one of two sites. Investment in plant and machinery has been minimal, due in part to the perception that this was a 'traditional', labour-intensive, low-skilled industry. In the past two years, profitability, sales and market share have been dramatically hit by cheaper imports from Asia. 'How can we compete with Indian producers, who are able to ship cotton gauzes at 4.1p a metre, when we produce it at 10p a metre?', was the question posed by the production director.

In response to a changing market place the new strategic direction of ABC plc was to concentrate on more state-of-the-art, technologically advanced products aimed at the medical market, rather than the mass production market. ABC plc needed to introduce change on an enormous scale and move to being a high technology, multi-skilled workforce. Having decided to rationalize on one site, introduce more advanced machinery, a different manufacturing 'cell' structure, team working and a performance oriented culture, ABC could not afford to have industrial disputes or indeed a workforce which was resistant to change. *What would you do in such a situation?*

ABC decided to take a bold approach: that this was an opportunity enabling them to set up a 'greenfield' site, to introduce new working practices and to set the course for the future. The starting point was:

> we want people who will fit into this new culture we are trying to create and we want people who are committed and who have the potential to work in self-managed teams.

The change process was started by running half-day workshops with teams of ten people, facilitated by team leaders. By getting shop-floor employees to look at the way they did things and encouraging them to be constructively critical, they were able to see how grossly uncompetitive they were. Having digested information on their relatively poor market share and poor profitability, along with information on industry 'best-practice' and what their competitors were doing, teams were asked to make recommendations on the way forward. Not surprisingly, with this level of involvement and commitment, the need for change was startlingly real, as was the sense of urgency. By building on the output of these workshops and linking it to the direction the board wanted to take the company, the *momentum for change* was created. Building the new vision and enabling employees to see it and be involved in it, however briefly through these workshops, led to a polarization of views, those who were all for change and those who rejected it. Surprisingly, there were few who were holding on to the middle ground. Those who wanted to work in this new environment had training and development programmes designed so that they could efficiently meet their business deadlines in the new environment. Those who rejected change were given the opportunity to discuss their concerns. An attractive package and career counselling was available to those who wished to go.

Case History 7.2

Easing the Pain of Transition: The Use of 'Modelling'

This is the case of a public sector organization which was 'forced' to adopt a far more commercial approach by the government's policy of market testing and more open competition. This government department (let's call it the property department), primarily responsible for valuing both public and private properties for the purposes of council tax and rent assessments, had up until a few years ago been guaranteed a large proportion of its work from government departments. With the advent of the Conservative party's drive to cut public expenditure, to open local government services to market forces and to improve service to customers, the message that was being sent out was that if the private sector could do the work more cheaply at a higher or equivalent quality and provide a better service, they would win the business.

Key changes which were required from the property department managers were: the need to be more commercially aware, to have a better understanding of customers' needs and requirements, better time and project management skills, being able to sell effectively, and to respond to tenders. Many of these issues meant a major shift for managers who prided themselves on their technical professionalism and their 'quality of work at whatever cost' approach. Understandably, there was a lot of unease and concern from managers on the direction the property department was taking and the impact this would have on them.

The property department's director of human resources arranged for all senior managers to attend workshops which 'modelled' the new future they would have to face. What followed was a series of five-day workshops attended by 15 managers at a time. The objective was to model as closely as possible the key issues managers would have to respond to in this new environment. Issues such as responding to tender bids, team work, presentation skills, strategic selling, managing the performance of staff, coaching and developing staff to respond to change were all built into the five-day event. Managers were encouraged to think about the key learning points for themselves, the changes that would have to be made at an organizational level and what they had to do to bring about this change. In addition, external presenters were introduced to impart 'best practice' in the private sector on areas which were relevant to their needs.

By 'modelling' what the future would hold for them and enabling managers to 'touch, feel and breathe' this new environment, the real-life change became less threatening and was tackled with a more concerted focus and energy than hitherto apparent.

Case History 7.3

The Psychological Cost of Change: What to be Aware of

In this section I would like to focus on the psychological barriers which inhibit change and what the manager needs to do to overcome them. This is a theme which is taken up by Professor Schein in an article published in the *Sloan Management Review*. He opens his article as follows:

> If you put a dog in a green room and give it electric shocks, it learns to steer clear of that room. But what if the green room is organisational change, and people are so afraid of past experiences with it that they won't try anything new?

The following are all fears which have to be overcome, before change can be effectively implemented:

Fear of failing others: this is a fear of failing caused by the anxiety of what others will say and do if desired outcomes are not achieved. This is the fear that Schein attributes to organizational blame cultures, which can inhibit innovation and change, because people are too fearful of finger-pointing and having their 'cards marked'. From a manager's point of view, this type of fear is most difficult to overcome. Removal of this type of fear will gradually come about as the culture of an organization changes and as it dawns on people that it is only through taking calculated risks, doing things differently and learning from mistakes, that improvements arise. Creating a supportive, rather than a blame, culture is the first step in ensuring this debilitating type of fear is eradicated. The organization as a whole, not just individuals, suffers from this type of fear.

Fear of failing oneself: this operates at a much more personal level and is a result of the individual's lack of self-confidence and perceived lack of ability. Training and coaching are often the best way to reduce this. Development centres can be valuable in countering this type of fear, as they create an environment where individuals can learn about their strengths and weaknesses in a non-threatening environment (assuming the development centres are being run for development and *not* assessment). By reducing an individual's feeling of inadequacy and accentuating the strengths they have, this type of fear can be relatively easily overcome.

Fear of the unknown: this fear is a result of having to work outside of one's comfort zone. 'I've never done it before ...; I don't know what to do ...; what if X happens, how will I cope ...', are the sorts of comments made by individuals suffering from this type of fear. Education and information can readily overcome fear of the unknown, as can 'shock therapy' – getting people to do things they are fearful of and letting them get so used to their fear, they no longer perceive it as threatening!

Fear of success: it may be hard to believe that fear of success could be an issue for some individuals, but it does arise. For some people, getting attention from failure is all they have known – we have all come across the hard-luck colleagues who, try as they might, always seem to get things wrong, have accidents or struggle to keep their head above water. For this type of individual this catalogue of disasters is a coping strategy, for whatever reason. Success would take away all the 'benefits' they get from failing.

KEY ACTION AND LEARNING POINTS

1. What have been the main learning points for you in this chapter? What do you need to do to act and build on them?

2. What are the key barriers preventing you as a manager from effectively implementing change? Are the people you manage sufficiently trained and supported to deal with what you will be/are asking them to do?

3. What aspects of 'best-practice' can you build into the change process, either from within your organization or from other organizations?

LEARNING POINTS FROM THE CASE HISTORIES

Many organizations embark on a change programme without fully considering the implications, especially the reactions of employees. The Case History describing the property department highlights how change can be implemented through 'modelling', ie recreating the new environment as realistically as possible. This enables individuals to touch, feel and breathe what their working environment will be like in the near future and helps them to learn in a non-threatening environment. If an organization can provide a 'living' model of the vision they are trying to create and then give employees the opportunity to appreciate what this will entail for them personally, the main threats to change have been overcome, namely: fear of the unknown and wanting to stay in the 'comfort zone' because that is their only point of reference.

The Case History on ABC plc highlights the importance of involving employees in creating the momentum for change. In this example managers were aware that the success of new working practices would depend on how readily employees accepted them and the involvement they had in defining them. By providing the business reasons for change and listening to the views of employees, the need for change was driven by 'wanting to be more *competitive* than competitors in everything we do'.

Finally, Case History 7.3 demonstrates how the debilitating effects of the fear of change should not be underestimated. By putting mechanisms in place to deal with fears, a manager can dramatically improve the chances of success.

SUMMARY

The business case

Managing change is not easy and has lots of risks and difficulties attached to it. However, mastering continuous change is critical for sustained competitive advantage. Any drive to improve the level of service to customers, be it through technology or changing processes, requires learning new behaviours and attitudes. New technologies and processes can not exist in a vacuum: it is people who at the end of the day determine how efficiently and effectively a business strategy will be implemented. Effective managers understand how to introduce and sustain change, causing minimum disruption to the business and getting early successes.

Putting it into practice

There are two parts to the effective implementation of change: preparing for change and the transitionary stage. In terms of preparing for change, three key elements need to be in place to overcome psychological resistance: creating the need for change; highlighting the benefits of change; and the ease with which change can be introduced. While this approach may take time, its effects will be enduring and help overcome individuals' fear of change. The alternative is to impose change, regardless of what others think. This, however, is a very short-term approach, where individuals are far more likely to resort back to past behaviour.

During the early part of the change process it is important that success is achievable and recognized, to give confidence in the new approach. In addition, people should be involved so that they feel they have a say in creating the new environment. Above all, the objective is to ensure that people's attitudes change and in turn their behaviours to the new way of doing things.

The key principles

For meaningful change to occur at the organizational and individual level, three phases need to be completed. First, the existing way of doing things needs to be questioned and analysed, so that more effective and efficient means can be evolved; this is known as 'unfreezing'. Second, the new way of doing things is introduced. This is the most critical stage, where problems and issues are most likely to arise. Finally, the benefits from change need to be consolidated, individuals and organizations need to evaluate where they have got to and how much further they need to go. This stage is characterized by confidence in what has been achieved and feeling that the storm has been weathered. This stage is referred to as 'refreezing'.

Chapter 8

ACHIEVEMENT FOCUS

Action is the rocket fuel that launches your vision
(Belasco, 1990)

WHAT YOU CAN EXPECT

After reading this chapter, you will have a better understanding of:

- why achievement orientation is important

- how organizations develop achievement cultures

- features which characterize managers who are achievement-oriented

- the key principles underpinning an achievement focus

- how achievement-focused organizations bring about real results

- the organizational factors which can inhibit an achievement focus

————— OVER TO YOU —————

1. On a personal level, how achievement-oriented are you? What factors help and hinder you in achieving results?

2. What are the main points you would like to get from this chapter?

3. How achievement-focused is the culture of your organization? What factors help and hinder the organization in achieving results?

4. How important or relevant is being achievement-oriented in your current role and to your business objectives?

THE BUSINESS CASE

Action. Being achievement-focused. Getting results. These are *critical* factors which count at the end of the day, if a business is to be a market leader. Successful organizations get where they are by focusing and clarifying their business objectives and then gearing the organization and individuals to achieve them. Both at the organizational and the individual level, being achievement-focused is imperative. Having a clear vision is important, wanting to be customer-oriented is important, looking to differentiate the organization from competitors is important – but *unless* this is translated into action, they remain just good ideas. It is through creating an organization which allows and encourages its employees to excel through action and achieving results that leading organizations are formed. Each department, each individual has a part to play in the success of the corporate body, and by focusing on outcomes and defining how those outcomes should look and feel, success is not far behind. Having an achievement focus is important for a business for the following reasons. Through being achievement-focused the organization:

– Learns

An organization is not dissimilar to an individual in the way that it learns. It is through trial and error, through putting things into practice, through exploring different options that genuine learning takes place. This learning is an important organizational *asset*. By learning what works and what is less likely to work, an organization is able to focus its energies on the former and be far more inclined to get results. Organizational learning only takes place through action, however, by doing and reviewing. Research indicates that successful organizations focus on achieving small but significant results in any new initiative. These organizations then build on and learn from these small projects, giving larger-scale projects a head start.

– Empowers

Fundamentally an organization is a collection of individuals. For the organization to succeed, therefore, it has to empower its employees to act for themselves. Successful organizations are flatter, respond much quicker to changing needs than their competitors and provide services which are of a higher standard and more innovative than their competitors. This can only happen if the organization empowers individuals to learn, grow, develop and perfect through action and by doing. Successful organizations are learning that by encouraging shop-floor operatives and people at the sharp end to be more achievement-focused, they are able to dramatically add to the 'bottom line'.

– Gets results

The success of an organization is dependent on its ability to get results: gaining market share, an increase in share prices, growth, profitability, customer satisfaction – are all reliant on energy and commitment. Those organizations which get results do so by mobilizing their resources to do things not just to average standards but to the highest standards. The bottom line is that only those organizations which have a clear focus on achieving ambitious targets and gear themselves to do so, build a sustained competitive advantage.

PUTTING IT INTO PRACTICE

What are the practical steps you as a manager can take to ensure you and your team are achievement-focused? This section will concentrate on achievement *behaviour* and on what effective managers actually do. The following five steps may be a useful guide:

1. Have a 'game-plan' and prepare your ground.
2. Aim for early successes.
3. Create an expectation of success.
4. Stick to your course of action, even when things are not going well.
5. Have a belief in yourself and in what you are striving to achieve.

1. Have a 'game-plan' and prepare your ground

For a manager to be achievement-focused, he/she needs a clear idea of what it is they are trying to achieve. The difference between managers who procrastinate and those who get on with it helps shed light on the essence of being achievement-focused. Procrastination comes through having too many ideas and having too many routes that one could follow; consequently indecision and lack of clarity impede performance. It is useful to use others as sounding boards, either informally or formally to get their ideas and thoughts on your suggestions. Elicit the pros and cons of different options. For some this process may muddy the waters even more; the message is not to expect an answer to jump out and hit you over the head. This process should enable you to gain sufficient information from which you can make some informed decisions. You need to be in a position where you have collected *all* the relevant ideas, so that you do not have to back-track later because you had not considered all the options. Having a 'game-plan' entails narrowing a number of options down into a clear framework. Notice how the emphasis is *not* on having clear answers, rather a clear framework. Having a framework allows you to have sufficient latitude to refine a course of action, based on new information and new requirements. The first rule, then, is that the 'game-plan' should be both *realistic*, *achievable* and defined as *specific outcomes*.

Before you can start implementing the 'game-plan', it is important that you prepare your ground. One way to prepare is to understand what managers in your organization actually do to achieve successful outcomes. Having this information can be extremely useful, as success behaviour is very often culture-specific. That is to say, what counts as success behaviour in one organization is not always seen as such in others. By preparing your ground you are in a better position to work out your tactics: what you want to achieve and how you will achieve it.

2. Aim for early successes

Clarifying your options and having a tactical plan are important steps in achieving goals. These options, however, need to be 'piloted' before a final choice can be meaningfully made. The process of piloting enables different options to be tested – eliminating what does not work is as important as identifying what does work. In many cases there are important learning points from failure – so long as they are seen as such. Some organizations fall into the trap of spending so much energy on laying blame that very few meaningful lessons are learnt (see the Personal View 8.2). There is a lot of evidence to indicate that many successful products and companies experienced early failure, but learnt critical lessons from it. Action and achieving early successes provides the 'green light' for decisions which hitherto were awaiting final confirmation. By minimizing risks, seeing at first hand what does and does not work, ambitious programmes can take root through small beginnings. Information from real-life data and achieving early successes is powerful in convincing and influencing others (see Case History 8.1).

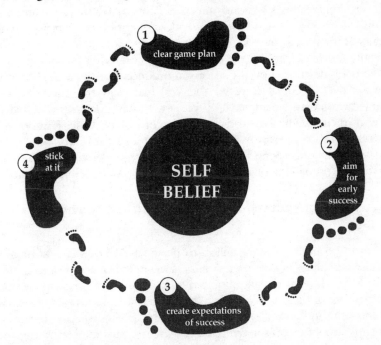

Figure 8.1 *Stages to achieving challenging results*

3. Create an expectation of success

Your role as a manager is important in orchestrating successful outcomes. Nothing creates an achievement culture as effectively as success. That is why the earlier stages referred to in this chapter are important: by defining objectives which are realistic and achievable, then testing them out and modifying them, you are creating an expectation of success. The soft issues such as 'the feel good factor' should not be underestimated if you are demanding a lot from others. Success in the vast majority of cases has to be worked for and therefore needs energy and fuel to feed it. Motivation, commitment and a desire to win are the human elements which enable difficult challenges to be overcome. If you can accentuate the positive and enable people to believe in themselves, you have created a powerful force which has a momentum of its own.

4. Stick to your course of action, even when things are not going well

Achieving results has a lot to do with being persistent and sticking at it. No doubt your organization is no different from many others, which are littered with well-intentioned projects which have fallen by the way-side. These 'failed skeletons' are often brought out into the public arena each time someone wants to do something different or creative. If you have gone through the three earlier stages – of having a clear plan of action, getting things moving in a small way and creating successful outcomes – this fourth stage will automatically fall into place. Persistence often provides the critical breakthrough which can dramatically transform a project or product. One of the key messages in a book entitled *Breakthroughs* is the importance of seeing things through to the end. The book describes how 14 successful products and services, such as the microwave oven, Federal Express, the Walkman and the anti-ulcer drug Tagamet, became such commercial successes, largely due to the persistence and belief their originators had in their worth (see Case History 8.1). Persistence in this context is not about following a particular course of action regardless; it is about having followed the other stages described in this chapter, so that the probability of a successful outcome is considerably increased.

5. Have belief in yourself and in what you are striving to achieve

Achievement focus is strongly linked to personal effectiveness. Without an inner drive and belief in oneself, it is difficult to mobilize energy and commitment for a task. In your pursuit of objectives you will come across many obstacles and points of view which offer a different course of action. Unless you have confidence in yourself and in what you are striving to achieve, it would be very easy to keep constantly trying different alternatives each time you encounter an obstacle. Self-belief – intuition or 'gut-reaction' that you are doing the right thing – is important in maintaining a course of action in the face of criticism and cynicism.

In conclusion, this section has addressed the three critical steps to achieving results: action, thinking and personal belief. *Action* provides the physical drive and energy to get things done; *thinking* provides the direction and context; while *belief in oneself* and the cause provides the inner motivation and conviction for a positive outcome to be achieved.

THE KEY PRINCIPLES OF ACHIEVEMENT FOCUS

What skills or personal attributes enable successful people to achieve their objectives? There are a number of responses to this particular question. One suggestion is that high achievers have 'Type A' personalities: individuals who have difficulty relaxing, are ambitious and competitive. They are strongly goal-oriented and want to win at any cost. Their competitiveness and desire to win make it difficult for them to forget about work at the end of the day. Burnout, or mental and physical exhaustion can be extremes of Type A behaviour. Type B personalities, on the other hand, are far more relaxed and composed. While they are ambitious, they do not have a 'win at any cost' mentality; they can keep their goals in perspective.

The Type A and Type B theory originated from work done on individuals who suffered from coronary heart attacks. Researchers felt there might be a correlation between the personality type of people who suffered from a heart attack and those who were less prone. After having completed extensive research on thousands of patients, the researchers concluded there was a positive correlation between Type A personality and susceptibility to having a coronary. Being achievement-focused without the checks and balances can be detrimental to physical and psychological well-being.

It goes without saying that achieving results is closely linked to having the *desire* and the *ability* to achieve goals. Figure 8.2 demonstrates the interrelationship between ability and the willingness to achieve results. Those in box 1 have both the ability and the desire to achieve results and are therefore exploiting the talent they have. These individuals can be used by organizations as 'champions' to try and convert those in boxes 2 and 3. Those in box 2 need to be 'switched on' – the reasons for them being 'unwilling' need to be identified and addressed; those in box 3 are willing but do not have the necessary skills or abilities to achieve. Our box 1s can act as mentors and coaches to the other two boxes. The major difficult with box 4s is identifying whether they can be moved into box 3 (in which case they have the potential) or if they are genuinely a 'lost cause'.

Finally, it is worth mentioning the 'thinking' processes which characterize achievers. There is now a growing body of evidence to suggest that those who achieve personal and business objectives have a greater range of thinking strategies which help them. The growth in popularity of neuro-linguistic

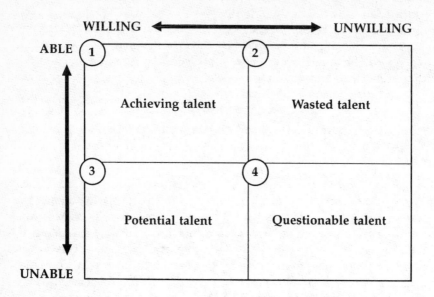

Figure 8.2 *Linking achievement orientation to ability and desire to achieve*

programming (NLP) is based on its focus on understanding the mental processes of high achievers. Similarly, much has been written on visualization and how high achievers, whether in business or sport, use creative visualization. The lesson from NLP and creative visualization is that effective people use thinking strategies which enable them to achieve. It could be positive self-talk; it could be imagining in every detail the delivery of a flawless presentation to the board or a large audience. Both NLP and creative visualization stress the importance of using both the right and left hemispheres of the brain, which control different cognitive processes. The left side of the brain is the rational, logical thinking part; while the right side is the more creative, intuitive side, controlling many of the sub-conscious processes. Far too many managers use only the left side of the brain, limiting their ability to think laterally and their potential to achieve creative outcomes.

Case History 8.1

What Enables Achievers to Achieve?

This section is based on Nayak and Ketteringham's book, *Breakthroughs*. The book describes how major breakthroughs in products and services were achieved. This section distils the critical features of the people behind these breakthroughs. Take the case of the CAT body scanner and the two men behind its successful launch: Godfrey Hounsfield, the inventor, and John Powell, the man brought in by EMI to provide the direction and the launch of the scanner. Hounsfield was driven by the vision of being able to scan the human body far more effectively than with x-rays: 'Once I realised that my method was considerably more efficient than conventional x-rays, I hoped to see things they could not possibly see. I must win in the end, was my general feeling'. Hounsfield not only had the technical skills and the ability to see the applications of his invention, but also had the resilience to overcome the many technical problems which would beset him. Indeed, it was this desire to tackle problems and a belief in his own competence which resulted in him seeing through a project where he was the only real driving force behind it. As the authors write:

> Hounsfield's biggest dilemma, after theory and technology had been worked out in his mind, was finding an audience that could partly grasp what he was talking about and also see that it served some necessary purpose. Doctors, who needed this technology, didn't understand it. Physicists, who could understand it, didn't need it.

The importance of a clear vision, belief in one's own competence and in the potential of the product, emerges in the story of 3M's Post-It notes. As the authors note, Spencer Silver – the person behind the discovery of the new polymer which had the special adhesive qualities – managed to convert the idea into a commercial reality by persistently selling the features of the adhesive to colleagues within 3M. 'I was just absolutely convinced that this had some potential'.

This vision and belief in what one is doing does, however, need to be converted into action and commitment. A feature of achievers is their ability to reduce big issues into smaller, more manageable processes. Hounsfield developed a prototype scanner with little investment, using the resources he had at his disposal. Another success featured in Nayak and Ketteringham's book is that of Taiichi Ohno, the inspiration behind Toyota's production system. It was his ability to get others to try his recommendations on a small scale, see the benefits for themselves and then convert others, which made him such an influential figure. Indeed, without his ability to get things done, the authors argue it is unlikely that Toyota would actually be the force it is today in world manufacturing.

A look at people who have achieved success reveals the following 'ground rules': have self-belief and conviction that what one is doing is right. Having the resilience and tenacity to overcome problems and persuade others is no less important. In addition, develop prototypes or projects on a small scale, which will provide you with the momentum to continue what you have started. Success breeds success.

Creating Achievement-focused Cultures

The very real challenge facing many organizations, especially those which are operating in a new competitive environment, is how to create a more achievement-focused culture? Many organizations, from Hospital Trusts opting out of the NHS, to government agencies and borough and city councils, are operating in an environment which is very different from what they have been used to. Operating in an achievement culture has several implications and may include one or more of the following: being far more accountable than in the past; having challenging targets and objectives to achieve; providing value to customers and end-users; working within a more stringently controlled financial environment and talking the language of profit and loss and creating competitive advantages.

So how are achievement-focused cultures created? I feel that an integrated approach is needed, where the way people are recruited, trained, appraised and rewarded reinforces the new culture. Before the journey to create an achievement-focused culture can begin, there needs to be some appreciation of where we are now and where we need to be, short and longer term. How critical the need to change is will determine how dramatic the culture change needs to be. It is as well to point out that when referring to an achievement-focused culture, it is not some utopian state. It would be more accurate to describe it as a 'state of readiness', which prepares the organization to assume a culture more in line with its corporate objectives.

So what does this mean in practice? Let's take the case of Halcyon City Council, which is operating in an environment where many of its services operate with 'market testing' or compulsory competitive tendering. The bottom line is that unless the services can compete with the private sector, the work will be offered to external contractors. Assume that for the past 10 years Halcyon City Council has had a very bureaucratic culture: not responsive to the needs of customers; layers of management who are involved in the decision making process; slow and deliberate in the way decisions are made, and managers achieving promotions through having avoided making mistakes, rather than actual achievements. The senior management team have over the past year or so been preparing for a more business-oriented environment. What should they be doing to make the workforce aware of this new culture they will be operating in? Here are five main steps they might choose to take:

Create change teams: a natural process, where teams can identify the main areas which need changing and can involve key people in the consultation and implementation stages.

Informal and formal communication: regularly communicate what needs to be achieved and what successes are being achieved. Use every opportunity to get your own message across, not the message of the 'doubters'.

Focus on changing behaviour: changing attitudes and beliefs takes much longer than changing behaviour. Behaviour is observable, quickly changeable, rewardable and reinforcable.

Aim for immediate successes: nothing reinforces new behaviours and an achievement culture as much as success.

Have a human resource strategy linked to achieving results: an integrated HR strategy which consistently rewards, develops and appraises people against challenging criteria is an important step in creating an achievement-focused culture.

KEY ACTION AND LEARNING POINTS

1. What are the key learning points in this chapter?

2. What are your personal objectives for your managerial career, short and long term?

3. What timescales have you set yourself to achieve your objectives; what resources will you require and how will you monitor your performance?

LEARNING POINTS FROM THE CASE HISTORY AND PERSONAL VIEW

Case History 8.1 identifies the features of the people behind major breakthroughs at EMI, 3M and Toyota. The people behind the breakthrough products all had several common characteristics: they were able to visualize how their 'inventions' could be used and applied in the market place. They were driven by an inner conviction that they were on the right path and, because of this self-belief, were able to persuade others. The Personal View 8.2 describes how organizations can make a start in creating achievement cultures. By focusing on changing behaviours and reinforcing them through human resource systems, the organization is sending out a clear message: these are the behaviours we value. Changing behaviours is more likely to result in changing attitudes and beliefs.

SUMMARY

The business case

An achievement focus is important if organizations and individuals alike are to achieve ambitious business objectives. An achievement-oriented culture positively encourages individuals to set ambitious goals, to learn from mistakes and to continuously expand the boundaries of what is possible. These organizations set the standard which others must follow. More often than not they demonstrate how dramatic improvements in business performance can be achieved by striving to achieve ambitious outcomes.

Putting it into practice

A number of practical steps can help bring about successful outcomes. Success can not occur, however, without the desire and motivation of individuals. Individuals who consistently achieve challenging objectives do so by having a clear idea of what they are striving for. They implement actions quickly, albeit on a small scale and use this as a 'springboard' to tackle more difficult goals. Perseverance in the face of adversity and a belief in themselves and the goals they are striving for are further characteristics of those who achieve results.

The key principles

Personality is an important feature which can characterize high achievers. Those with Type A personality are often tense-driven, set themselves ambitious goals and are self-motivated to achieve them. High achievers are also more likely to use a greater variety of thinking strategies in the way they approach and tackle issues. They are likely to be creative and see new possibilities and opportunities in the problems they work on.

Section 4

GETTING THE BEST FROM OTHERS

S = Software contains a questionnaire relevant to this area

Chapter 9

TEAM WORK

We would rather have a team of stars, than a team with a star
(Jackson, 1993)

WHAT YOU CAN EXPECT

After reading this chapter, you will have a better understanding of:

- how teams can add value to a business

- how you can create a winning team

- your role in ensuring the team achieves results

- what differentiates a good from a poor team

- your own team style

- the theory and practice of team work

- how organizations create winning teams

Refer to the software for an insight into your team style.

OVER TO YOU

1. What are some of the issues regarding team work in your own organization or department?

2. What are some of the organizational factors you need to change to create effective teams, and what would be some of the benefits of doing so?

3. How would you describe your own team style; what are the main contributions you typically make in a team?

4. What are the business drivers creating the need for team work?

THE BUSINESS CASE

Team work is a critical factor in gaining competitive advantage. The need for team work arises from external factors, such as:

- more intense competition
- faster response times
- more frequent and ever-faster development times
- ever-increasing 'added value' being offered consumers.

In brief, the business case is that the introduction of self-managed, multi-disciplinary teams enables organizations to compete far more effectively, flexibly and innovatively than before. Team work is becoming *the* way for organizations to respond to the changing needs of customers. The value of multi-skilled, self-managed teams is that they have the authority and responsibility to introduce more efficient and value-added processes and, through sharing information, learning from mistakes and innovating, ensure continuous development.

Given that team work is evident in every facet of business life, small improvements in the way teams are selected, managed and rewarded would have quite a major impact on the effectiveness of board meetings, shop-floor team meetings, management meetings, project meetings and problem-solving and brainstorming meetings.

In today's flatter organizational structures, team work provides the means by which companies are better able to meet their responsibilities in a highly competitive market place. With the introduction of new technologies, new working practices and faster response times, organizations have to 're-engineer' processes in line with these changes. Team work is a relatively easy and cost-effective way of making a dramatic improvement in the performance of the business. These benefits to the business can be further improved by re-engineering an organization along the lines of project teams who collaborate and work together for the life-time of a particular assignment. Once that project is complete, team members disband and form different teams. In so doing, they provide a mechanism for organizational learning, for best practice to be cross-fertilized and help remove organizational barriers such as lack of trust and poor communication, which can be symptomatic of functionally oriented organizations.

In short, teams are able to create value: they can provide a flexible, cost-effective and innovative way to manage a business – especially one going through transition.

PUTTING IT INTO PRACTICE

Effective teams do not develop by chance – a manager has an important role in shaping their success. The following points may be useful in creating successful teams.

The 'soft' issues

Without *trust* and *collaboration*, a team can not exist. A collection of individuals working together may be a group, but not necessarily a team. What differentiates the team from the group is that the former *shares* information and work because their effectiveness depends on everyone pulling together and supporting each other. This trust and collaboration creates an environment where a true exchange of ideas and learning takes place. A team is only as strong as its weakest link, and all team members need to feel they belong to, and are valued by, the group as a whole. This trust and collaboration enables team members to give each other the necessary feedback and support so that each individual member gives their all and maximizes their contribution to the team.

Empowerment is a much-used word, but it is critical for a team to perform effectively. Without *self-sufficiency* to make decisions and without the necessary skills to respond to problems, a team would soon lose its credibility and motivation. The role of the manager is important in ensuring that the team is *multi-skilled* and does not have to keep referring upwards or to external sources each time it encounters an obstacle. Alongside the necessary skills, the team needs to be encouraged to reach decisions for itself and, where appropriate, to challenge and question traditional ways of doing things which impede the team's effectiveness. Empowerment, therefore, encapsulates having the necessary skills to address real issues, as well as the authority to see actions through (see Case History 9.1 for further information).

It is also important to note that senior management support is critical if teams are to have an impact outside of their areas of responsibility. A project team, for example, will probably want to correct the cause of a problem, rather than have to keep dealing with the symptoms. As such, it would most probably have to recommend ways in which problems could be prevented, to managers in other parts of the business. Senior management *sponsorship*, therefore, is critical if the team is to genuinely address business issues and not superficially tamper with them. Even if the team comes up with decisions which are likely to be controversial or difficult to implement, there needs to be unconditional commitment to consider them seriously.

The final ingredient in developing an effective team is open and regular face-to-face *communication*, both within the team and externally, so that others are aware of what progress is being made and what impact it will have on them. Communication within the team is critical, so that concerns can be aired before they become major issues. A philosophy of open communication means that anyone in the group can voice any concerns or suggestions on the direction of a particular project. Healthy debate and constructive feedback are positive outcomes of an open communication philosophy (see Case History 9.3 for additional features of effective teams.)

In summary, a manager's role is critical in creating the right environment for the team to thrive. The following conditions are important:

- they are a cohesive unit, working for each other
- the right skills are inherent in the team
- communication is open and constructive
- the team has the authority and responsibility to deliver real benefits
- the team has the support and backing of senior managers.

The 'hard' issues

To develop effective teams, other, more tangible, factors need to be considered. For example, how viable would a team be if individuals were rewarded and remunerated according to their individual performances, as opposed to the performance of the team as a whole? Rewarding just the individual performance could prove to be quite divisive and engender internal competition and mistrust. While rewarding teams has a number of inherent problems, the philosophy is far more conducive to effective cooperation. In fact most teams would prefer to be judged as a team, rather than a collection of individuals and to be rewarded as such (Case History 9.2 gives a broader perspective on this point).

Second, teams need to be given 'real time' within which to operate. If a team is required to work on a specific project in their own time, or when they can get time off from other commitments, the outcome is predictable. As a manager, therefore, it is important to arrange for all team members to work on achieving their objectives within realistic timescales and with realistic resources.

A third point closely linked to the previous one is that the team must be *located* as a single unit. From my experience, expecting a team to function effectively when they are in separate geographical sites is a recipe for failure. Working in close proximity engenders a feeling of belonging, encourages open discussion and debate, and prevents the sense of frustration that nothing is happening.

Helping teams through their development cycles

Teams go through different stages of development and place different requirements on a manager at each stage. John Adair (1986) has described four stages through which all teams must go while they strive to achieve their goals:

1 forming
2 norming
3 storming
4 performing

It is worth looking at these stages in more detail. Figure 9.1 describes four development stages, which correspond to Adair's.

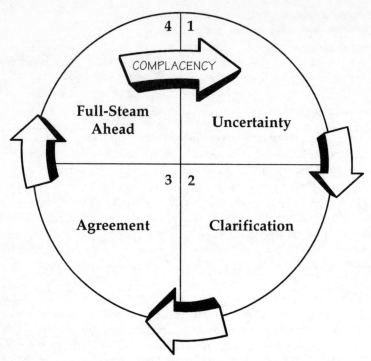

Figure 9.1 *A typical team development cycle*

1. Uncertainty

At this stage most of the concerns of the team members are directed towards understanding the task and how the team is made up; it is directed primarily to collecting information. The focus of attention is likely to be around basic issues such as:

- terms of reference for the team
- who is the leader
- what is expected of individuals
- what sort of behaviour will be appropriate.

2. Clarification

During this stage the team begins to review the information collected at the previous stage. The validity of the task or qualifications of individual members, including the leader, are usually challenged at this time. This is often quite an emotional stage in the team's development as individuals and/or sub-groups strive to steer the team in the direction they feel most appropriate. It is also here that interpersonal conflicts can arise. This phase is very important as it forms the basis of how the team members will operate in the future. The team here is often concerned with questions such as:

- what roles do team members want to fulfil?
- how qualified are team members to deliver results?

- does the team have enough of the right resources?
- is the task and its timescale practical?
- how well do team members work together?

3. Agreement

At this stage the group begins to harmonize. The potentially disruptive emotions and energies of the clarification stage become more cohesive. The team gains a better understanding of how the various individuals can work together towards common goals. In those groups where conflict will be a constant feature, due to personality, methodological or ideological clashes, then procedures begin to emerge for dealing with the conflict. The team is likely to consider:

- the mission of the team
- formulation of plans for achieving the objectives
- standards to which the team members will operate
- how the team will deal with conflict, internal or external.

4. Full-steam ahead

By this stage the team should be sufficiently clear about what it is going to do, how it is going to do it and what its strengths and weaknesses are. It should be able to deliver the 'promise'. Individual roles begin to be seen in terms of getting the tasks done. Flexibility and support develops as the members begin to understand each other and build up rapport. The cohesiveness of the team begins to be reinforced by achievements on the task.

Complacency

It is often the case that after a team has been performing effectively for a while it becomes complacent. In this phase the team goes into a semi-automatic mode of operation. This is partly due to the success of the team's operating procedures. Teams in this stage of development are often unaware that the environment of the task might be changing. It is during this phase that the team slips into 'groupthink', where team effort is devoted primarily to maintaining the stability of the team. During the complacency stage teams can be overtaken by events and lose their vitality. However, if the team is to continue it will need to reform, perhaps take on new members and go back around the cycle described above. The team will look at itself and decide how things have changed:

- are the team's terms of reference different?
- does the team need to do things differently?
- what is going to be different?
- does the team need new skills and knowledge?

and so on until the team has once again gone through the uncertainty—clarification—agreement—full-steam ahead stages.

It is possible to get through the above stages quickly and with minimum disruption by ensuring that everyone is clear about:

- **roles:** who is going to do what and how are they going to do it?
- **goals:** what are the individuals and the team going to achieve, and by when?
- **procedures:** how is the team going to achieve its goals, to what standards, and how will it deal with conflicts, make decisions and monitor its progress?

══════ KEY PRINCIPLES OF TEAM WORK ══════

Probably the most influential work on team building is that of Meredith Belbin (1981), often referred to as 'Belbin's team types'. The premise underlying his work is that personality is as important a contributor to effective teams as the expertise and skills that individuals have. His work revealed that effective teams comprise individuals who *complement* each other and bring different qualities to the group. This is an important finding, in that most teams are often formed on the basis of technical expertise – be it a project team or a 'permanent' team. In the latter case, many boards are built on technical specialisms, eg finance, human resources, operations, sales and marketing, with very little consideration being given to the personal 'blend' of team members. According to Belbin's team theory, a board or team comprised predominantly of monitor-evaluators will be good at identifying the flaws in others' ideas and action plans and not be good at seeing other possibilities or how to overcome the objections. This is the classic case of *paralysis by analysis*. Equally, a team of highly creative, intuitive 'plants' (see Figure 9.2) will come up with lots of ideas, but not have the objectivity to narrow down their options and focus their energies on one or two core ideas. This is the classic case of *'pie in the sky'*: lots of innovative ideas, but not rooted in reality. This type of 'stereotypical' profile of the unbalanced team has many permutations, depending on the make-up of the group. The eight different team types are described in more detail in Figure 9.2.

Belbin came to his conclusions following research with teams attending management courses. His initial view was that the more intellectually able the team, the more effective they would be in solving issues. Selecting people by their scores on ability tests, he put together team 'Apollo', a group of intellectually able individuals. Unfortunately, this group did not perform well on the different tasks they were set. The team could not agree amongst themselves on the best course of action to take, and while they were very effective in intellectualizing a problem, they were not effective in coming up with a solution. When Belbin experimented with different group compositions, he discovered that the personality of team members was as important as their team role. It would not be a contradiction in terms, for example, for a finance director to undertake finance responsibilities as well as being the person in the team who ensures that conflicts between team members are resolved amicably.

In short, Belbin and others have highlighted the importance of getting a well-balanced team of individuals together, who can complement each other and 'add value', not only in terms of their technical skills but also their personal contribution.

Coordinator: as the name suggests, this is the person who undertakes the role of:

- clarifying what is expected of the group and therefore establishes goals and objectives
- prioritising the key areas the group need to address
- helping group members clarify their roles and responsibilities
- acting as a sounding board, summarizing the main conclusions and action points emerging.

Shaper: the key role is to shape, clarify and drive forward objectives and recommendations, so that there is sufficient clarity for the group to progress forward. This role, therefore:

- shapes and defines objectives and responsibilities
- tries to find a shape/theme emerging from the team
- pushes the team towards agreeing decisions.

Plant: is the role which 'plants' ideas and provides the group with 'fuel' in coming up with new recommendations to overcome problems and difficulties. The main roles of the plant therefore are:

- to generate ideas and suggestions in resolving problems/difficulties
- building on others' ideas and suggestions, or
- providing completely 'contrary' ideas and views to the consensus view, forcing the group to consider alternative options.

Monitor/Evaluator: the critic or devil's advocate best describes this role. The monitor/evaluator critiques suggestions and forces the group to think about their course of action, through:

- analysing problems and situations
- seeking clarification, and
- addressing obscurities.

Implementer: this role is the one most concerned with how the ideas and proposals are to be implemented and therefore brings a very pragmatic approach to the team. The implementer:

- reviews ideas and suggestions in terms of how practical they are to implement
- uses common sense in suggesting how plans might need to be modified.

Team Worker: this role emphasizes the need for the team to work together cohesively. The most important features of the team worker are:

- encouraging and supporting other team members
- attempt to resolve conflict in the team and attempts to reduce tension
- bring other people in to the discussion, so that there is a team contribution.

Resource Investigator: this role attempts to be the main interface between the team and the external world. It is this role which acts as the 'ambassador' for the team:

- acting as a go-between, linking the team with external agencies, engaging in negotiations on behalf of the team.

Completer/Finisher: this role is most concerned with ensuring all the small print has been checked, dates have been agreed and nothing has been overlooked.

- ensures dates, timescales and objectives have been clarified
- looks at the detail to ensure everything has been checked
- ensures that everyone knows what is expected of them to achieve the results.

Figure 9.2 *A summary of Belbin's team types*

Case History 9.1

Team Work in the Automotive Industry

Modern production lines are only as good as the individuals who assemble the cars. The adage that a chain is only as strong as its weakest link is epitomized in technologically advanced, just-in-time, modern manufacturing. Hi-tech tools are only adding value if their users are well trained, can solve problems for themselves and are capable of reaching decisions, without constantly having to refer upwards – which describes the Japanese automotive giant Toyota. Toyota began production in the UK in early 1993, with team work being one of its underlying philosophies. Over 1,000 staff work at the Burnaston site, in Derbyshire, producing the Carina E. A team comprises four or five members working together, supervised by a team leader who then reports to a group leader. The teams have a particular responsibility, but they are given the opportunity to improve the process, however they see fit, as part of Toyota's 'kaizen' philosophy of seeking continuous improvement. As Brian Jackson (1993), Director of Human Resources, said in an interview with *Personnel Management*, the company is not looking for particular experience or qualifications, but for a certain type of individual: 'We want somebody who likes to work in teams and someone who can operate in a "constant change" environment'.

In his book, *Thriving on Chaos* (1988), Tom Peters cites the case of Ford's Team Taurus in the United States. This is an example of using teams in a wider sense, and forming multi-disciplinary teams to design and produce a car, using a completely new approach and concept. The traditional way of manufacturing a car at Ford started off with the designers working on an outline on paper and giving it to the engineers, who then worked on how to make it. They in turn would then pass their plans on to the manufacturing and purchasing people. In the chain of events, the next team of people to be brought into the equation would be the production plant. Then came marketing, the legal and dealer service departments, and finally the customers. According to Peters, 'if a major glitch developed, the car was bumped back to the design phase for changes'. The new approach was to bring all the disciplines together, and do the whole process simultaneously as well as sequentially. The manufacturing people worked alongside the design people, sales and purchasing, legal, service and marketing. The result was a process which even Ford was surprised with: better cars, greater innovations and a process which was resulting in wholesale 're-engineering' – not just tinkering around the edges.

Case History 9.2

A Sector Ripe for Team Work

The financial services sector has come in for a fair degree of criticism in the last year or so. Banks, building societies and life assurance companies are competing with each other to try and get a bigger slice of the lucrative pensions, PEPs, and life assurance market. Team work should have been an important element in the way these organizations operated and the lack of it has arguably been an important contributory factor in the poor press they have been receiving. Most of the organizations in the sector operate a branch network, where a branch is responsible for a geographical area and is run by a branch manager, who has a team of sales consultants reporting into him/her. Team work would be particularly important for the banks and building societies, where individuals at the counters provide leads to the sales consultants. Cross-selling and the benefits of team work are strategically very important for the business.

The problems that have occurred

The main problems facing the banks, building societies and life assurance industry have been:

- in the main, poor customer satisfaction
- poor persistency rates (ie, people surrendering their policies within a few years of taking out the policy) due to poor advice
- a high turnover of sales consultants
- ineffective cross-selling, due to a 'them and us' mentality
- attracting and retaining the right calibre of sales consultant
- individuals being promoted to managers, purely on the basis of their income generation as sales consultants.

The causes of many of these problems

People issues lie at the heart of the points detailed above, which stem from a number of causes. One is the philosophy of individualism being promoted over team work. In nearly all cases sales consultants are rewarded on their individual sales figures, rather than a system which takes into account both individual and team performance. The potential benefits of team performance over individual performance are:

- greater collaboration and sharing of information
- the creation of a supportive environment.

A team culture is far more conducive to a quality, customer-oriented ethos. For a start, financial advisers are encouraged to talk about 'our' customers, rather than 'my' customers. The onus is on building a longer-term relationship with customers, rather than the mentality of a 'quick' sale, because sales figures happen to be poor this month. Indeed, many of the banks and building societies have begun to move towards this team culture, and are supporting it through relevant training, a guaranteed basic salary and team performance bonuses. Other financial services are reluctant to leave 'the good old days' behind them, for fear of losing their star salesmen and the financial benefits they bring the organization, and have tentatively set up a two-tier salesforce: salaried and commission-only. This seems to be a prime example of internal processes coming before what is best for the customer – a team-oriented, customer-focused, professional sales force.

Case History 9.3

Creating Winning Teams

This case history is a compilation of 'best-practice' team-building incidents, from organizations the author has worked with; it is the story of Pete McGrath, a line manager with Abco plc. Pete was given the task of creating a project team to implement change within a manufacturing organization. His task was to identify areas where costs could be reduced by 20% in the manufacturing process *and* to recommend how changes in working practices could most effectively be implemented. The major change that would affect most people on the shop-floor was a new 'cell' structure, where a team leader would be responsible for a small team of 'charge-hands'. The role of this team would be to work on their individual production projects, being responsible for problem solving, decision making and monitoring their own performance.

Pete was astute enough to know that without the involvement of his employees, implementing change would be an up-hill struggle. He therefore created teams at different levels: a working project team, which had the ultimate responsibility on policy, and smaller implementation teams, led by members of the bigger project team. His primary task in getting together the project team was to have individuals who would:

- have credibility with people on the shop-floor
- have relevant technical skills, and
- provide a balance in the decision-making process.

Having got the team together, he clarified the objectives and the timescales they were required to work to. Each team member was asked to comment on the objectives they were trying to achieve, what they could bring to the team in helping to meet those objectives and on the barriers they felt would impede them. In facilitating this process, he achieved a consensus on how the project objectives would be achieved and the contribution each member would make. He 'gelled' the team further still by highlighting how each team member could complement each other: 'Jo, you commented how one of your strengths is coming up with new ideas and ways of solving problems; it seems to me that Bethan's objectivity and analytical skills will be important in helping you narrow down your options to those which are most practical'. By *removing potential barriers*, such as not having time-off from their full-time duties to work on the project team; by *clarifying objectives* and getting their 'buy-in'; by putting together a *balanced team* and providing them with the *authority* to reach decisions, Pete created the beginnings of a *winning team*.

KEY ACTION AND LEARNING POINTS

1. What have been the key learning points for you in this chapter?

2. What are the main steps you need to take to create effective teams? What are the timescales you are working to and what are the potential barriers?

3. What short- and longer-term steps do you need to take to introduce self-managed teams effectively; what will be the short-term benefits which will provide momentum to the process?

Learning points from the case histories

The case of Toyota's new manufacturing plant is evidence of the importance Japanese manufacturers place on team work and self-managed teams. Similarly, Ford in the USA has benefited from introducing team work in the design and manufacture of cars.

Introducing team work is not always an easy option. Case History 9.2, for example, shows how the finance sector has put forward a number of reasons why individual performance is more important than team performance, eg 'our most effective performers are strong individualists, we do not want to risk losing them'. The point that 20% of employees bring in 80% of the revenue is often used to justify not introducing team work. However, just think of the benefits to the organization if that 20% could improve the performance of the majority, through team work, coaching and development.

It is important that team members 'buy-in' to the objectives they are trying to achieve. There is nothing worse than team members going through the motions, trying to achieve objectives they feel are 'pie-in-the-sky'. In the case of Pete McGrath at Abco, he not only got the buy-in of team members, but also collected their views on what they could most effectively contribute to the team. By focusing on how different team members could help each other, and the strengths that different team members bring, Pete created an environment where individuals were being encouraged to actively participate and support each other.

SUMMARY

The business case

With organizations facing ever-more competition, many companies are relying on effective teams and team work to bring about a competitive advantage. Self-managed teams have the remit to define objectives and need to be given the authority to reach decisions that will enable them to achieve challenging targets. Self-managed teams should have the ability to monitor their own performance and call in different members to complement the core team wherever appropriate. Where teams work in parallel and there is an interchange of team members, the benefits to the organization are many:

- clearer lines of communication
- sharing of knowledge
- greater trust
- greater collaboration.

Putting it into practice

To create winning teams, both 'hard' and 'soft' factors need to be taken into account. Hard factors are the 'hygiene issues' that need to be in place before effective team work can take place, for example:

- rewarding team members on the performance of the team as a whole

- ensuring team members have 'barriers' to performance removed
- team members are physically located as a single unit.

In terms of 'softer', people issues, teams will function effectively if:

- they have senior management commitment
- there is open and regular communication and genuine trust amongst team members
- objectives are clear and the team has the authority to reach a decision in order to meet their objectives.

The key principles

The principles on team work emphasize two main points:

- effective teams have individuals who undertake different roles
- personality is key in matching individuals to roles.

Effective teams do not rely purely on technical skills, but contain individuals who are capable of undertaking a number of roles: from directing the group to ensuring team members are working effectively together. Individuals are likely to be predisposed to different roles, based not on their functional roles but on their personal characteristics. An important part of a manager's work in getting together effective teams is to match an individual's strengths with particular team roles.

Chapter 10

COACHING AND DEVELOPMENT

Coaching is face-to-face leadership that pulls together people with diverse backgrounds, talents, experiences and interests, encourages them to step up to responsibility and continued achievement, and treats them as full scale partners and contributors

(Peters and Austin, 1985)

WHAT YOU CAN EXPECT

After reading this chapter, you will have a better understanding of:

- what the key features of coaching and developing are

- what makes for effective coaches

- why coaching is important

- how you can become a more effective coach

- the psychological principles underpinning coaching

- on-the-job development strategies

OVER TO YOU

1. How competent are the people you manage; how would you describe their main development needs?

2. How often do you provide on-the-job development for your team?

3. What are the main points you hope to acquire from this chapter?

4. In what types of situations do you see coaching and development having a real impact on the business?

THE BUSINESS CASE

Coaching and development are *vital* parts of any business. Indeed, it could be argued that they are a *critical* means by which an organization ensures that it does not repeatedly make the same mistakes and errors. An effective way for an organization to learn and share information is through consciously reviewing key learning points. This is what lies at the heart of coaching and development: a dynamic process, which focuses on doing things better, more effectively and intuitively – through learning. Its value is not in telling others what to do, but in getting people to learn for themselves through creating new paradigms. The business case for coaching and development can be considered from a number of perspectives; two are described here.

The learning organization

In Chapters 1 and 2 you will have read how several leading organizations use core competencies as a means of differentiating themselves from their competitors. Organizations such as Sanyo have mastered miniaturization techniques, much as 3M, Kodak, Honda and many more have built their reputations and market shares around specialized knowledge.

Knowledge, however, is useless to an organization unless it can be applied, utilized and provide a competitive edge. Coaching and development enables this knowledge to be shared and spread throughout the organization. Through coaching, knowledge becomes accessible to all. Corporate knowledge continually evolves and remains even when key individuals move on. Organizations which anticipate and react to change proactively are those which continually advance their knowledge and change paradigms. Learning organizations create environments where employees at all levels are encouraged to try new ways of doing things, to learn from mistakes and to share this information with others, so that a continuous improvement chain-reaction is set in motion.

Managing change

Coaching and development are also of great significance in an ever-changing business environment. The issue faced by many organizations is, how do we minimize resistance to new working practices? For many individuals fear of failing or fear of the unknown are the barriers to change. Coaching and development are practical ways to overcome these problems – by providing individuals with knowledge and guidance which enables them to achieve difficult objectives. It is a method which delivers quick and often impressive results, where the recipients of the coaching and development get instant feedback on performance. Through coaching, individuals share their experiences with others, thereby dramatically improving the others' learning curve and the time it takes to achieve competence.

=========== PUTTING IT INTO PRACTICE ===========

A number of factors need to be in place before a manager can be thought of as an effective coach; these are:

1. Creating the right environment.
2. Having the right motives for coaching.
3. Managing by example.
4. Inspiring confidence.
5. Enabling development.

1. Creating the right environment

Coaching can be considered as the art of helping people to learn. Learning, however, does not take place in a vacuum: the right conditions and environment need to be in place. Coaching will thrive in an environment where individuals are motivated to learn, where it is seen as an on-going process and where everyone is receptive to giving and receiving constructive feedback on performance. Part of creating a coaching and learning culture is enabling people to learn from their mistakes, without blame. Indeed, learning cultures view mistakes as ideal learning opportunities.

As a manager, therefore, you need to encourage people to keep improving, to think of better, more efficient ways of doing things. Start off by asking individuals to give you feedback on your management style. Many organizations already employ a system where coaching is made easier through all-round appraisal systems. This system asks bosses, colleagues and subordinates to comment on an individual's performance. As giving and receiving feedback is a skill and, like any other skill, has to be developed, it is usually necessary to provide training programmes to create the right environment for coaching to thrive. In one City Council individuals were afraid to try new initiatives or to question why things were done the way they were because the organization had a long track record of blaming others if their initiatives failed. As one training manager commented: 'Fear of blame is our biggest barrier in getting people to take risks and be entrepreneurial, which is critical in the commercial environment we work in'. (Case History 10.1 includes more information on creating learning cultures.)

2. Having the right motives for coaching

A key requirement for effective coaching is integrity and sincerity. Some people could regard advice and direction from a colleague or subordinate as threatening. 'Coaching' could be used as an excuse to put people down, through finding fault in whatever they do. Integrity means genuinely having the best interests of the individual at heart. Sincerity is also important, in ensuring that not only is the advice given for the right reasons but in a manner which is 'acceptable' to the individual.

No distinction is being made between coaching and counselling, for the two share very similar characteristics. The counselling side of coaching applies to helping the individual recognize that they have a problem in the first place and one which is caused by their personal style. For example, a team member might be very good in their technical capacity, but alienate team members through their abrasive nature. A good coach would first get the individual to recognize they have a problem and then get them to think about how their interpersonal style could be improved. The effective coach does not point out individuals' short-comings, but works with them to explore the range of alternatives they have available to them.

Having the right motives ensures that things happen at the individual's pace, not the manager's; and it means the interventions introduced are right for the individual and not because they are most convenient for the manager.

A final point is that coaching and development should be seen as a two-way process, one where subordinates can approach their manager and offer suggestions on how the manager's style impedes them or the team. By genuinely believing in the worth of continuous development, one of the strongest messages a manager sends out is: 'There is always room for improvement and the responsibility to do so rests with all of us. I am willing to receive feedback on the areas you feel I perform well in and where you feel I am less effective in'. (For more information on the role of effective coaches, see Case History 10.2.)

3. Managing by example

Managers lack credibility and therefore effectiveness as a coach if they are not considered competent in what you do and do not live by coaching principles. There is often a double standard that managers adopt: do as I say, not as I do. It is a simple truth that unless you set the standards and your team have confidence in your abilities as a manager, you will not hack it as a coach. Where you make mistakes or errors of judgement, it is important to share these with those for whom you act as coach. Focus on the positive learning points and how these can be applied in the future.

4. Inspiring confidence

It is important to appreciate that both the coach and the person being coached have different needs. As a coach you need to feel that your views are valued. The recipient of the coaching needs to feel they are actually making progress and benefiting from the coaching. Inspiring confidence and accentuating the positive are important for this to happen.

Inspiring confidence can be done in two main ways: first, by providing new learning opportunities and communicating that your reasons for doing so are because you have confidence in the individual's ability to deliver what is being asked of them. Second, to review projects once they are completed, to talk through what the main learning points have been. To complete the learning cycle, you and the subordinate should have programmes in place which will address any development needs through coaching, self-development or more formalized training. (See Case History 10.3 for further information on the psychological principles of coaching.)

5. Enabling development

There needs to be a recognition that coaching skills will need to be supplemented with actual training and development for the subordinate. As a manager, for example, you may find that team members are too often fire-fighting and do not make contingencies for events until it is too late. You could spend a lot of time with them, making them aware of what they are doing well and less well and providing learning opportunities. However, if the team has not had fundamental training in project management skills, for example, the impact of your coaching will be limited. Under such circumstances it may be appropriate to run more formal project management courses for team members. However, coaching and development go hand in hand – the effects of the one are dramatically reduced without the other to complement it.

THE KEY PRINCIPLES OF COACHING AND DEVELOPMENT

A key principle here concerns the way people learn – a critical feature of coaching and development. Perhaps the most influential psychologist on the subject of learning is Kolb and his work on *experiential learning*. Kolb (1974) puts forward the idea that learning takes place in our everyday experiences and that we learn most from key events in our lives. He cites four key stages to experiential learning:

Experience: this stage uses experience as a learning process. The individual observes and reflects on the consequences of action in a particular situation. Experiencing new situations and new events is important if learning is to be an on-going process. New experiences generally bring about new ideas, thoughts and approaches. Through experiences we are able to reach new levels of understanding.

Understanding: this is the second stage of experiential learning, where the impact of experience enables understanding to be formed or re-formed. At this stage the individual begins to appreciate key learning strategies: through doing A, I can achieve B.

Planning: following on from understanding, the third stage is planning. Learning takes place at a conscious level, where individuals have to plan and think about what they need to do to achieve outcome A. The analogy can be made of an individual who moves to a new town and has to consciously plan their route to get from home to work. Within a matter of days, this route can be covered on 'automatic pilot', where the individual does not have to consciously think about it. Planning is a prerequisite to acquiring understanding.

Action: this is the culmination of the earlier stages of experience, understanding and planning and entails putting into action the new strategies.

This learning cycle is of relevance to the coaching manager for the following reasons: first the model provides a structured approach to learning. The model highlights how an individual needs to be exposed to new experiences; understand what the learning points have been; plan accordingly for the future and act on this new insight. Coaching encourages an individual to reflect on the quality of their work and the success of their interventions. The experience of *reflecting* enables individuals to be more objective and critical of their own work and over time enables them to understand new patterns and new ways of a better understanding of doing things. This in turn leads to what *planning* and coordinating needs to be done. Through the coach the individual gains greater insights into effective strategies for future situations and eventualities. By putting their re-learnt behaviour into action and beginning the learning loop again, we have a situation of ongoing refinement and improvement.

Case History 10.1

Corporate Coaching and Development

Corporate coaching in the context of this case history is the process by which an organization ensures critical knowledge is passed on to others. Without this transfer of knowledge, creating a competitive advantage would be extremely difficult if not impossible. Here we will focus on the '*what*' and the '*how*' of knowledge transfer.

First, *what* types of key learning points do organizations need to ensure get passed on? The human side of mergers and acquisitions is one such area. Take the case of Halcyon Electricity, which in its drive to become a supplier of 'energy' – gas and electricity – acquired Gas Co., a small independent gas company. The acquisition would complement the services Halcyon already offered its main business users and help win over other business users who relied on gas rather than electricity for manufacturing processes. Having spent several million pounds on the acquisition, Halcyon sold it 18 months later to an overseas energy company. The 'forced' sale resulted from a number of factors: insufficient preparation of how both the gas and electricity sources would be marketed; how the two companies' information systems, management teams, and client portfolios would be integrated; and how Halcyon should position itself in the market place. A major factor behind the decision to sell, however, was that the management teams operated in very different cultures. Gas Co. had a very informal way of operating and saw itself as entrepreneurial. Halcyon, however, believed in being very cautious but saw how this could be debilitating in a fast-moving market place. The truth of the matter was that it was not sure what type of culture it should be adopting and this uncertainty was not helping in its dealings with Gas Co. Halcyon's tendency was to agree one thing at joint managerial meetings, but then revert 'back to type' once it had considered all the information. It was imperative Halcyon *learnt lessons* from this acquisition, to prevent similar errors of judgement in the future.

How then did Halcyon begin to learn lessons from this experience? One means was through the internal consultancy division which had been initiated by the chief executive. This internal consultancy was a 'trouble-shooting' team, comprising individuals who had experience of strategically important projects. Indeed, the value these consultants provided to other parts of the business was such that 'failed' projects were seen as 'test-cases' from which others in the business could learn valuable lessons. The consultancy team was contactable via a 'help-line', so that line managers could discuss any issues and concerns on projects they were managing. Halcyon also recognized that it was managing many different businesses: its core electricity business; new ventures such as the gas business; and entering new markets both at home and oversees. It realized that each of these different businesses needed to have its own culture to compete effectively, given how cultural incompatibility was a key factor in the failure of the Gas Co. acquisition. In short, through a number of initiatives, ranging from that the company had to learn from mistakes to the setting up of an internal consultancy team, Halcyon ensured that key lessons from its failed acquisition were disseminated to other parts of the business.

Case History 10.2

The role-model Manager as Coach

This case history concerns 'John Steele', a composite of managers who have been identified as role-model coaches by their organizations.

John is the head of business development with the Midland Gas Company and has 35 people reporting to him, most of them young business graduates. In a highly competitive energy sector, John's department sells gas to large business users. The key elements of the business process are to establish a relationship with the key accounts through thoroughly understanding their business resulting in putting together a 'supply package' which is attractive to the client, meeting their short and longer term energy requirements.

John is aware that he can not afford to lose business and market share to his bigger rivals. He is also aware that clients may question the credibility and business awareness of his young team of account managers. At an early stage of their development, John began to introduce weekly workshops, based around actual clients' needs, and the threat being posed by competitors. The key as far as he was concerned was not to tell them what to do, but to get his team learning for themselves. By doing so, they would be in a much better position to anticipate problems and deal with them before they occurred. Coaching for John meant enabling his team to think for themselves and to evolve better, more innovative solutions to the needs of customers. His competitive strategy was based on adding value to customers through:

- understanding the clients' business better than the competition, and
- offering tailor-made, flexible, energy solutions.

From his point of view adding value did not entail competing on price. His workshops encouraged team members to think about the following: identifying the buyers and decisions-makers they needed to get close to; the knowledge and information they needed to assimilate to be able to talk confidently on the issues they faced; the clients' longer-term energy requirements; and what their own strengths and weaknesses were which could hamper or assist them in achieving their business objectives. By forcing team members to think about issues they had not yet encountered, John was using his personal experience to dramatically reduce the learning curve his relatively inexperienced team would have to go through. He also knew how important it was for clients to have the 'comfort' factor that the individuals they were dealing with were not learning on-the-job and at their expense. Hence the ability to recall events and success stories from past projects was important. John provided his team members with the challenges needed which would help them with personal development; he encouraged self-development and saw 'mistakes' as essential for learning. He was aware that his team would inevitably make mistakes, but did not want to inhibit them by creating a culture where mistakes labelled people as having failed. The business stakes were high, and coaching provided a mechanism by which team work, open communication and best practice thrived.

Case History 10.3

A Psychological Perspective of Coaching and Development

To understand what differentiates the highly successful job-holder from the less successful, psychologists often use what are called 'critical incidents'. This entails asking job-holders detailed questions on the way they approach their work, so that a clear picture begins to emerge on how they think, act and feel when completing successful assignments. By understanding thinking processes, psychologists can then use this information to pin-point the processes behind effective performance. Differences in performance can often be put down to thinking more laterally, being prepared to take risks, thinking things through more logically and systematically, rather than differences in actual knowledge.

This process, of understanding what successful job-holders do, lies at the heart of effective coaching and development. An effective coach does not tell people what to do, but presents different scenarios: 'What would happen if you were to do this, as opposed to this?' or, 'In what situations would that approach work and under what situations would an alternative approach work better?' The manager can bring these questions to life, by recalling personal 'critical incident' events, for instance:

> In the negotiation I had with XYZ plc, the critical process was convincing the client that we could meet their requirements just as well as our bigger competitors. I had anticipated how this would be the most difficult issue during the negotiations, so I took along with me performance figures which were relevant to their needs. I did not want to leave such an important issue to chance, so was prepared with this information. I also knew that he was someone who was liable to change his mind and 'sit on' things, rather than make a clear decision. For this reason, I knew I had to to persuade him and get his commitment in writing there and then.

The manager as coach therefore needs to be aware of the thinking processes used by effective performers and how to impart this information most meaningfully to others. A key principle of coaching is to act as a 'guide', helping people to become more aware of their thinking processes in the situations they do well in and those they do less well in. Through providing alternative strategies, the coach can begin to instil a belief that the individual is not bound to do things the way they have always been done. Indeed, this is a much underrated function served by coaches – getting people to continuously evaluate the way they do things. In a business environment where change is a constant, it is important that people learn to adapt through self-insight. Part of the coach's role is to get people to appreciate that fundamentally they are helping themselves. If they feel the coach is doing things for them, there is likely to be a strong element of reliance. By accepting they have learnt for themselves through facilitation by the coach, they are far more likely to transfer their learning to new areas.

In short, coaching relies on a number of *psychological* principles: getting people to appreciate that there are usually far more effective and efficient ways of approaching problems. By encouraging individuals to review their own performance and seeing what they do well and less well, areas for improvement can be identified. Resources and energies can then be focused on development by understanding the strategies and approaches used by star performers.

KEY ACTION AND LEARNING POINTS

1. What have been the main learning points for you in this chapter?

2. What will you be doing differently in the way you manage and develop others and how will this difference be evident to others?

3. What cultural and organizational 'barriers' to effective coaching and development need to be removed in your business?

LEARNING POINTS FROM THE CASE HISTORIES

Organizations need to set the pace in encouraging learning and self-insight – through creating learning cultures. In the case of Halcyon it was important that critical points from the forced sale of its acquisition were learnt. In a market place where it had to compete on new fronts and in new markets, its commercial viability depended on being able to shorten its learning curve. The stock market, customers and employees would soon lose confidence in a company which was not able to manage change and repeatedly made the same mistakes.

Case History 10.2 highlights how managers can add value to the business and customers through coaching and development. A key feature of effective coaching is encouraging individuals to acquire more varied and innovative 'thinking strategies' through handling new on-the-job assignments. Through coaching and development individuals are able to dramatically reduce the learning curve.

Case History 10.3 provides more psychological perspectives on coaching. The key point here is that getting people to learn new paradigms cannot necessarily be formally taught. The value of coaching and development is in encouraging individuals to critique their own performance and to learn from past experiences.

SUMMARY

The business case

Coaching and development are important in a business environment which is geared to doing things better, more efficiently, quicker and cost-effectively than the competition. Continuously 'adding value' to customers is a key business differentiator. This chapter suggests that coaching and development are a viable and practical way for knowledge and information to be shared throughout an organization. They are the means by which genuine learning can begin to take place. The real value of coaching and development is that they occur on-the-job and in real time – they are the building blocks of adding value.

Putting it into practice

Effective coaches share a number of core characteristics: they create an environment where learning is encouraged, where feedback is welcomed and the focus is on wanting to do things better. Without this environment of 'learning', coaching and development would be perceived as threatening: 'I can't be very good at what I do; why else would my manager be helping me so much?' The coaching itself needs to be conducted in partnership, where manager and subordinate provide each other with constructive feedback and learn from doing so. Coaching is definitely not the manager telling the subordinate what to do – even though the manager may well have 20 years' worth of experience and have seen it all before. The confidence individuals gain from coaching and development is important for ongoing learning. Equally important is the role of the manager in ensuring their own behaviours are reinforcing the right messages.

The key principles

Coaching and development are a means of getting individuals to learn for themselves. Kolb's model of experiential learning is a useful guide; it structures learning into four key stages: experiencing new situations and learning from them, which in turn enables an individual to plan for new situations and new experiences so that desired outcomes can be achieved.

Chapter 11

LEADERSHIP

Great necessities call forth great leaders
(Bennis and Nanus, 1985)

WHAT YOU CAN EXPECT

After reading this chapter, you will have a better understanding of:

- what the main features of leadership are

- why leadership is important

- appropriate leadership styles

- the relationship between leadership and power

- situational leadership styles

- how leaders differ from managers

- how to apply the principles of effective leadership

For an insight into your leadership style, refer to the software.

———— OVER TO YOU ————

1. What would you like to acquire from this chapter; what are the issues you are facing?

2. In your organization, what aspects of leadership are effective and less effective?

3. How effective is your own personal style of leadership? What opportunity have you had to demonstrate leadership?

4. What features of leadership behaviour have you seen in different managers that have impressed you?

5. How are you (or might you be) able to demonstrate leadership in your current role?

THE BUSINESS CASE

One of the main criticisms levelled at managers by their subordinates is that they provide no leadership, no direction, no sense of purpose or vision. *Leadership*, at both the macro and micro level is critical to 'sell' the *vision*, to inspire and instil confidence. At its most fundamental, leadership is critical if an organization is to achieve challenging objectives, be it at the board level or on the shop floor. Successful organizations have managers who lead by example and who provide a sense of direction; they take people with them, not by force, but with personal charisma, clear and effective communication and with the energy and commitment they put into their cause. Leadership is far more than a 'nice to have' characteristic, for the following reasons.

Creating the vision

In today's increasingly competitive market place, managers need to demonstrate 'thought leadership'. Having clarity of thought and direction is an important means by which the organization is able to differentiate itself from the competition. Thought leadership is not about tinkering with processes at the edges, but introducing wholesale, radical and innovative changes. Thought leadership is about having a compelling and challenging view of the future, where the boundaries of what is possible are continually being stretched.

Making the impossible possible

While 'thought leadership' provides the vision at an intellectual level, this needs to be brought to life by leadership behaviour. Leadership behaviour is about winning *hearts and minds*. The role of a leader is critical in energizing others to accomplish difficult and challenging objectives. The *commitment and passion* behind your message will determine the business results you get.

During times of uncertainty and transition, people look towards the leader for clear direction. Espoused values and beliefs need to be backed by behaviour and action – one without the other will not 'wash'.

Effective leadership is about making the impossible possible.

PUTTING IT INTO PRACTICE

As a manager, what are the basic principles of effective leadership which you need to put into practice?

Two of the more important ingredients that go to make an effective leader are *self-confidence* and having a clear *strategy* on direction and deliverables. A number of issues are interrelated with self-confidence and strategy, so let's look at each one in turn.

1. Strategy

A leader must have a clear vision of what they want to achieve and a strategy for doing so if they are to be effective in accomplishing challenging goals through others. The Personal View 11.3 highlights how a clear vision and a plan of implementation enabling the vision to happen are critical features of effective leaders. A leader, whether head of a division, the shop floor or the entire organization, needs to be clear in the direction and objectives they are striving to achieve. Decisive leadership is likely to be even more critical for organizations undergoing dramatic change, brought about by the need to become more competitive. Strategic leaders closely link change programmes to:

- the needs of customers
- how the organization will differentiate itself from the competition.

Strategic leaders have an excellent understanding of the market place they compete in and continuously look for ways in which they can add value to customers. Leading change based on the needs of customers is a highly effective way of mobilizing others' energy and commitment – it clearly focuses the mind on the real external issues rather than the inward politics. Clarity on direction and the way forward are so important for employees, who look for reassurance and confidence from managers.

2. Self-confidence

A leader needs *self-confidence and conviction*. Leading others is not an easy course: people need to be convinced and persuaded if they are being asked to make sacrifices and begin a difficult journey. Being half-hearted or lacking real conviction will be easily picked up by others. Unless a leader can convey their goals and ambitions for the business with clarity and an unshakable conviction, others will remain detached. This detachment and lack of enthusiasm is a major obstacle to the effective implementation of challenging assignments. Case History 11.1 further demonstrates how important self-confidence is in decision making and in handling difficult situations.

3. Consistency

Gaining others' commitment for a particular course of action will not happen overnight. It is important to keep repeating a message at every opportunity so that it becomes a feature of people's working lives. The chief executive of a financial service company consistently repeated that customer satisfaction was the key to their future success. This was not an easy message to get through given the profits made by many financial institutions in the late 1980s with apparently minimal customer focus. However, slowly but surely the point was getting across, not just because it was regularly made, but also as key performance indicators were linked to how well the business and and its employees were achieving customer satisfaction. Like many leading customer-oriented organizations, Birmingham Midshires Building Society has built its vision around 'exceeding customers' expectations', a message which is consistently reinforced in everything the company does: in the way it rewards, develops and recruits employees.

4. Actions speak louder than words

Nothing conveys more commitment to a cause than *action*. If customer satisfaction is a critical differentiator, then make sure that barriers impeding this goal are removed. Create an environment which places more emphasis on the customer than internal politics. In the case I was referring to earlier, the chief executive moved all financial consultants to a salaried basis from commission, because he felt this was more conducive to ensuring that the needs of customers came before the personal needs of the consultant. Indeed, from the employees' point of view this was a most significant and dramatic move in demonstrating how important customer orientation was for the business. The actions of senior executives are so important in reinforcing key messages. In one FMCG company the drive towards greater team work and more open lines of communication became empty words when board members were regularly criticized for not being more forthcoming with key information and did not demonstrate collegiate behaviour.

5. Devolve authority and responsibility

Effective leadership is dependent not only on how objectives are achieved but also on how they are formulated. Just as charisma, energy and drive are key characteristics of leaders, so too is the ability to 'switch' people on by allowing them to take responsibility for their actions. An important factor in leadership, therefore, is achieving results through others. Devolving authority and responsibility means a lot more than telling and delegating. It means providing individuals with information on what you are trying to achieve, getting their *involvement, consulting them*, but ultimately allowing others to reach decisions for themselves and providing them with the authority to see them through. Leadership is the art of *empowering* others to achieve organizational objectives, through providing a compelling *vision* and by the *actions* you take. As you can see from the Personal View 11.3, 'switching people on' through articulating the vision is important if others are to then take responsibility for implementing objectives.

6. Communicate regularly

In many of the points which have been covered so far, communication is an important underlying theme. Action, credibility, creating the vision, empowering people – are all heavily reliant on regular communication. Keeping people informed on what you are striving for, how the organization is performing,

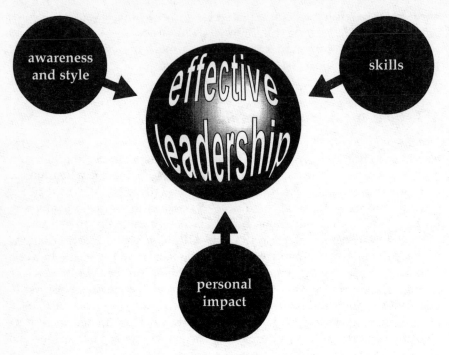

Figure 11.1 *Aspects of effective leadership*

sharing successes, are all bound up with communication. Even though employees are unlikely to be involved in formulating decisions concerning the overall running of the business, there are many positive benefits which come about through providing them with regular communication on broad business issues. One important psychological benefit is that people actually feel involved with what is happening and subsequently more committed to the aims and objectives of the business. Regular communication can dispel myths and rumours which can sap the energy needed to drive forward ambitious projects. Regular two-way communication can also prove to be a very constructive way for fears and concerns to be aired and for preventative actions to be taken. Regular team briefings, newsletters and company forums are ways to facilitate two-way communication. Having elicited feedback, mechanisms need to be in place, to deal with major concerns – failure to do so will cause resentment and is likely to result in those concerns being magnified to such an extent that they prove extremely difficult to deal with later.

In short, effective leadership depends on a number of factors, demonstrated in Figure 11.1 and highlighted in this section. Without the right skills, an ability to win others over and achieve results, leadership will not exist.

THE KEY PRINCIPLES OF LEADERSHIP

Much of the theory of leadership is not radical or new. Perhaps the research cited most often is Blake and Mouton's Managerial Grid. Blake and Mouton (1964) adapted the key findings of researchers at the Universities of Ohio and Michigan into leadership qualities. Their research indicates that two of the most meaningful dimensions which constitute leadership are:

■ people orientation, and
■ task orientation.

The authors conclude that individuals tend to have a preference for one or the other dimension. A focus on people orientation indicates the leader gets things achieved through their personal relationship with others. A strong emphasis is placed on establishing trust and ensuring that interpersonal issues get resolved quickly. Harmony and a well-motivated work force are the main goals of the people-oriented leader. The task-oriented leader, as the name suggests, places more emphasis on getting the job done; they are likely to be focused on the demands of the job, the objectives and timescales. Blake and Mouton have built on this basic model to describe how leaders can be categorized depending on the degree to which they are high or low on the task/people orientation scales.

A further refinement of the Blake and Mouton work can be found in the work of Hersey and Blanchard (1982). Their work puts the task and people orientation in the context of how 'mature' the subordinates are. Maturity is defined here in terms of both technical competence and psychological maturity. This information will help determine the most appropriate leadership style – a point highlighted in Figure 11.2, and discussed in Case History 11.2.

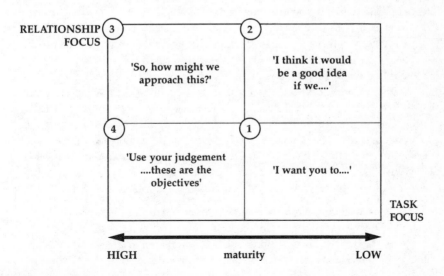

Figure 11.2 *Situational leadership*

High task/low relationship (1) leader behaviour is referred to as 'telling' because this style is characterized by one-way communication in which the leader defines the roles of followers and tells them what, how, when and why to do various tasks.

High task/high relationship (2) behaviour is referred to as 'selling' because with this style most of the direction is still provided by the leader. He or she also attempts through two-way communication and support to get the followers to 'buy into' decisions that have to be made.

High relationship/low task (3) behaviour is called 'participating' because with this style the leader and followers now share in decision making through two-way communication and much facilitating behaviour from the leader, since the followers have the ability, maturity and knowledge to do the task.

Low relationship/low task behaviour (4) is labelled 'delegating' because the style involves letting followers 'run their own show'. The leader delegates since the followers are high in maturity, being both willing and able to take responsibility for directing their own behaviour.

Case History 11.1

Leadership on the Shop Floor

This case history is intended to stress how leadership is as important on the shop floor as it is in the boardroom. This case history is put together from 'critical incident' interviews carried out with two 'blue-chip' manufacturing organizations. Both organizations were restructuring the shop floor to devolve more responsibility to operatives. As part of a selection and development programme, both clients wanted to 'benchmark' the characteristics of effective operatives. By focusing on the critical aspects of a particular project, and analysing the interview transcripts, the differences between the more effective and less effective job-holder can be drawn out. From the interviews conducted I have put together some of the *leadership behaviours* characteristic of successful operatives. For reasons of clarity, I will summarize many of these interviews in one individual – Melinda.

Melinda is well respected by team members; she may not always be popular, but is seen as having a clear focus on what she wants to achieve. There are some things such as *improvement orientation* and being *customer-oriented* she will not compromise on. Indeed, these subjects are regularly, almost religiously, mentioned at meetings. The reason she is so well respected is that she would not expect anyone else to do what she personally would not do. Her *commitment* to these goals is complete and she spends time listening to other team members on how processes and structures can be made more effective and efficient. You see her regularly making notes on the ideas and suggestions that people make.

What makes Melinda stand out from the others, however, is that she *makes decisions and acts* on the information given her. Her way of working highlights the fact that leadership does not necessarily equate with power – leadership is taking other people with you, changing things which are hampering performance and making difficult decisions when they have to be made. She communicates clearly and makes her point in a way where you can't but help agree with what she says. She is thorough and logical in the way she conveys points and then asks for your own opinion. She has a very *non-threatening style*, where she can respond to your doubts without belittling you. I think what I really like about her is that she will admit when she has overlooked something or is talking on a subject matter she is not that familiar with.

Melinda is a very *self-confident* individual; she has no real need to be liked and consequently can make decisions without worrying how others will look upon her. Take the example that happened last week, where the shift manager was asked to make some cost savings and decided to get rid of four part-time staff. Melinda persuaded him not to, as the team worked well and the four part-timers were good performers. She went back to him, having talked to other team members, and presented him with an alternative solution which centred around reducing wastage (and hence cost) from a particular process. She also draws a fine balance between being a team member and being a team leader and does not get into situations which would compromise her doing her job to the best of her ability.

Case History 11.2

Is Situational Leadership the Full Story?

There is no single style of leadership which is effective in all situations – this is the premise of situational leadership. So, for example, in a fire-fighting situation a no-nonsense leadership style would be more appropriate than a more consensual style. However, the point I wish to highlight in this case history is that one's effectiveness as a leader is also determined by *knowledge* and *experience* of the market place one is working in. Leaders do what they do because they have learnt that in situation A, strategy B is usually effective, if implemented by a C leadership style.

Take as an example the case of an assessment carried out where two utility companies were merging their high street shops to create a new entity. The bigger partner in this merger asked if I would assess the two managing directors, with a view to identifying which one of the two was most suited to the position in the new company. The first step was to look at the business plan for the newly-formed company, NewCo., so that I had a better understanding of what the new MD was required to achieve. This was followed by a meeting with the chief executive to establish the personal characteristics he was looking for that would enable the MD to achieve the ambitious business objectives. Clear and decisive leadership, vision, flair, entrepreneurship were some of the features describing what the chief executive wanted from the new MD, to enable the business to grow and expand in a very competitive market place.

Having put both respective MDs through an assessment process, assessing them on a range of managerial competencies, it emerged that we had two very different people. The one whom the client chose to appoint, based on several interviews and a detailed managerial assessment report, was the more entrepreneurial of the two; let's call him John.

What transpired was that John was made managing director and within six months or so was experiencing a number of difficulties, primarily compounded by the fact that in the space of 18 months – from the time the business plan was completed to the present – the market place had dramatically changed. Competition in the high streets was bordering on the ridiculous, with offers of buy now and pay in six months and interest free payments. *The only way NewCo. could compete was to dramatically reduce its cost base, and fast.* This was not the area in which John was at all confident. He had built his career on being innovative and using an 'offensive', entrepreneurial style of leadership. What the business required at this time was a more 'defensive', 'cost-leadership' style. While John was competently directing the company in extremely difficult times, he was having to go against 'the grain', contra to the knowledge and experience which had enabled him to get where he had.

Confidence acquired through having worked in a variety of business environments is a key element of an effective leadership style. Leadership style, therefore, needs to be responsive to the differing needs of the business. Without a range of leadership styles (both people- and business-related), an individual can only have a limited impact.

Personal View 11.3

Are Leaders Born or can they be Developed?

My own view is that leaders can be developed in all but one important area – the *visionary*. There are certain arenas where the expectation of the audience has to be met, the classic being politics. It does not matter how good your views are, how determined or sincere you are, if you can not get your message across forcefully and appeal to the heart as well as the head, then you will only be partially successful. The visionary leadership style is required where a company or country is in a state of confusion and *needs* and *wants* guidance, direction and conviction from their leader. The words 'needs' and 'wants' have been emphasized – the distinction is that a company may need guidance and clear leadership but employees may not *perceive* that to be the case. In such circumstances they have no great expectations of their leader nor do they expect them to be highly visible. In the case of needing and wanting clear leadership, nothing other than a visionary will do. In times of difficulty and adversity the great visionaries have shone through: Martin Luther King, Mahatma Gandhi, Nelson Mandela, Churchill, Hitler, all have led with authority and personal charisma and *met the expectations* of their 'followers'.

In industry, two people come to mind who fit the requirement of fulfilling the expectations of their followers – Richard Branson and Anita Roddick. Branson, for example, lives up to his image of being innovative and entrepreneurial by his unconventional dress sense. Like very few other chief executives, he is seen 'on-the-job' – on his planes serving customers with drinks and asking them about levels of service and satisfaction. Similarly, Anita Roddick's leadership embodies her values of supporting the communities from which many of her products originate. Both Branson and Roddick are *living the visions* they believe in. My view, in short, is that this type of leadership is innate, rather than learnt – you can not learn to be a visionary leader.

Other types of leadership, such as '*cost*' and '*thought*' leadership can be taught. The majority of leaders fall into one of these two categories. Take Archie Norman, for example, who turned around the ailing supermarket giant Asda. His background as the finance director of the Kingfisher Group and a McKinsey consultant was no doubt critical in the effective implementation of tight cost controls and a competitive strategy which would allow Asda to re-establish itself as a dominant force in the retail industry.

A further factor which I have not yet touched on which is important in leadership can be referred to as '*believability*'. Part of the reason why Asda share prices rose was because the City *believed* Archie was the right person for the job and probably the most important reason for Tony Blair winning the Labour leadership. Believability, however, will soon dissipate without *credibility*. Credibility can only be demonstrated once the individual is in a leadership role, while getting there in the first place has a lot to do with believability.

KEY ACTION AND LEARNING POINTS

1. What have been the main learning points for you in this chapter? What do you need to do to act and build on them?

2. What have been the main points of interest for you on the software regarding your leadership style? What does this tell you about where your leadership style will be effective and less effective?

3. How high a priority is developing leadership skills? How will developing leadership help you in your current role and in your future career?

LEARNING POINTS FROM THE CASE HISTORIES

The main points from the case histories are that effective leadership relies on behaviours and actions supporting the vision. On the shop floor and in the boardroom leadership relies on a consistent set of behaviours such as having the self-belief and confidence to make difficult decisions and being prepared to be unpopular. It also relies on being fair and having integrity, on involving others and providing them with the authority and responsibility to achieve challenging objectives, as described in Case History 11.1. Effective leadership is also dependent on, for example, 'thought' and 'strategic' leadership. In the case of NewCo., the managing director's leadership style was heavily reliant on being entrepreneurial but lacked a 'cost leadership' strategy, which was what was required by the business at that particular time.

Finally, leadership qualities have to do with behaviour, and leadership behaviours (like most other behaviours) can be *learnt*. The exception, however, is likely to be the 'visionary' leader, an exceptional individual, whose drive comes from values, beliefs and convictions which, while immensely personal, have a profound impact on others.

SUMMARY

The business case

Leadership is critical if organizations are to achieve ambitious *business objectives*. At the board and shop-floor levels leadership qualities and behaviour are imperative, especially in organizations undergoing difficult changes. Effective leadership embodies the main values which the organization is attempting to cultivate – whether it is to be more entrepreneurial, or exceeding customers' expectations, people look to leaders to demonstrate these behaviours and actions.

Putting it into practice

Leadership in practice is heavily reliant on two qualities. First, a leader needs to have a clear *vision* of what they are trying to achieve. It is this clarity which enables effective leadership decisions to be made in the midst of chaos and uncertainty. *Self-confidence* is the second quality which effective leaders require. If you do not believe in what you are doing and have faith in your abilities, no one else will either. It is the confidence and passions – which can only come from within – which enable 'hearts and minds' to be won over.

At the end of the day, leadership is not a theoretical concept but a dynamic entity. Leadership is action; it is about achieving challenging objectives through others and providing people with the means to continue doing so. Ultimately, effective leadership is about getting things done through others, not by being autocratic and telling, but by involvement, providing authority and giving others responsibility for their own actions. Effective leaders enable leadership to be cascaded to others.

The key principles

Leadership is situationally-based: different styles are needed for different situations. Leadership style is heavily influenced by the personal characteristics of the leader, the people they are managing and the nature of the situation being managed. These factors determine whether 'telling', 'selling', 'participating' or 'delegating' is the most appropriate leadership style.

Chapter 12

MOTIVATION

The drive to win is motivated from the inside out
(Waitley, 1994)

WHAT YOU CAN EXPECT

After reading this chapter, you will have a better understanding of:

- how and why motivation is important in the work context

- factors which create satisfaction and dissatisfaction

- what a manager's role is in creating a motivating environment

- how business performance and motivation are linked

- how motivation means different things for different people

- organizational factors which create satisfaction

- the theory and practice underlying motivation

Refer to the software for an insight into your levels of motivation.

——— OVER TO YOU ———

1. How high a priority for you is motivating others and why is this so?

2. How personally motivated are you? What effect does this have on your ability to motivate others?

3. What factors motivate you and which factors are demotivating? What does this tell you about your needs and how do you see these changing in the future?

4. What organizational factors influence motivation and what can you do to either harness or reduce these factors?

THE BUSINESS CASE

A fundamental feature of successful organizations is a well motivated workforce. Motivation is so important, because it affects so many areas of work:

- productivity
- quality of work
- commitment
- sales figures
- culture of the workplace.

Motivation is currently highly important to organizations because of change 'How do we manage the day-to-day business, as well as introduce change, without demotivating people?' For many organizations, change is a constant and is not always conducive to creating a motivated workforce – many people find it threatening and are tentative about ongoing change. Only through motivating people to want to change can a *desire and the commitment* for it be created. In the work environment motivation is generally created by individuals having *clear goals* (not job descriptions), feeling capable of achieving them, and having a clear idea of what the desired outcome is. Successful organizations and successful managers appreciate how overall performance is inextricably linked to the motivation of individuals. Get the motivation of individuals right and other things will tend to fall into place.

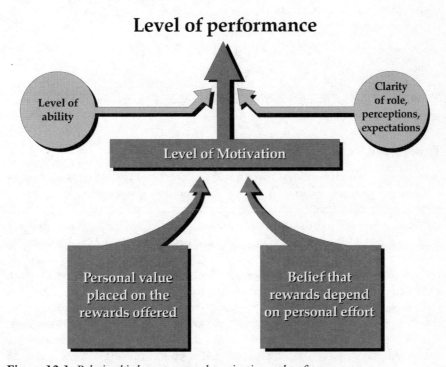

Figure 12.1 *Relationship between reward, motivation and performance*

The second strand to employee motivation is the changing paradigm of rewarding people. Historically, high performers have been rewarded through promotion up the career ladder. With many organizations cutting out managerial levels, this motivational route is likely to be less available. The challenge, therefore, is to maintain levels of motivation in an environment where traditional motivators such as a promotion, seniority and the trappings which go with them are no longer the order of the day.

By rewarding individuals based on their 'added value' to the business and creating an environment where results and not one's position count, an organization has the beginnings of a paradigm shift. The opening quote, then, has an important message, namely, that motivation is fundamentally highly personal to the individual and relies heavily on perception. In other words, if individuals perceive that the organization is valuing them, if they feel that they have a future with it and it in turn is giving the individual feedback to that effect, the chances are the individual will be motivated. Effort and commitment are strongly linked to benefits, eg job satisfaction, challenging assignments, recognition, etc. Put another way, there is a strong causal relationship between how motivated an individual is and the value they will provide the business. Find out what enthuses and motivates people, try and meet those needs and you will have individuals trying new, more creative and innovative ways of doing things. The ultimate aim of the organization should be to create an environment where the needs of the individual are continually being met, through regular two-way communication.

PUTTING IT INTO PRACTICE

As a manager, what are the things you should be doing to motivate your employees? The following practical steps are based around psychological and environmental issues.

1. Involvement

Few things stifle motivation more than imposing tasks and dictates on subordinates. Involvement of subordinates in the decision-making process is critical in generating the energy, commitment and motivation, to produce high quality work. How often do you see individuals simply going through the motions because they have been told down to the last detail what to do. Involvement is as important for the manager as it is for the subordinate: after all, most subordinates know more about their particular area of responsibility than their manager. Involving the subordinate therefore provides a sense of *purpose*, a feeling of being *valued* and that 'my views and thoughts matter around here'. Involvement is also important from the point of teamwork. If subordinates feel that everyone is pulling in the same direction, on an agreed course of action and have had a say in determining that course of action, there is strong motivational desire to make things work.

2. Responsibility

Another strand of motivation is providing individuals with responsibilities outside their comfort zone. Whereas some individuals will be daunted by responsibility, those who are both able and willing will thrive on this confidence shown in them. Giving subordinates responsibility sends out the message: if you are good enough, this organization is prepared to recognize that and leave you to get on with it. Responsibility can take several forms, but the main one is allowing individuals to reach their own decisions, to deal with problems and issues using their best judgement, without constantly being monitored by their manager. Achieving objectives which are *challenging* is an important motivator for individuals in its own right. Creating a working environment which individuals find motivating does not have to be an elaborate or complex process. The point was made earlier that, fundamentally, motivation is about *matching* the needs of the organization with the individuals. If individuals feel they are 'growing' and developing and at the same time contributing to the success of their team or department, this can be an enormous motivator, providing other factors are in place. Case History 12.1 gives more on this.

3. Delegation

Delegation is another important constituent in ensuring a motivated workforce. People feel motivated by the fact that their boss is prepared to spend time coaching them on a subject outside of their 'comfort zone'. I deliberately use the term 'comfort zone' to indicate the fact that delegation should not be seen as 'dumping' work one does not enjoy on to subordinates; it should be mentally challenging and broaden the job-holder's role. New and challenging work, as we all know, is a good motivator – because it provides *job satisfaction*. The fact that one's manager spends time explaining what they require of an individual and highlighting potential problems and pitfalls is gratifying in itself. We all like to be noticed and recognized after all. Delegation in itself, however, is not a motivator. Just imagine if your boss came to you and gave you a list of things to do on their behalf, but failed to clarify what they wanted doing, by when, and didn't define the authority you had in ensuring the work was completed.

4. Recognizing good performance

A good definition of a manager is: '*an individual who gets the best from others*', and of course there are numerous ways in which this can be achieved. One of the best and simplest ways to get the best from others is recognizing when they do a task well. Such recognition is, however, relative to the individual's capabilities. So, for example, if your secretary who is normally prone to making typing errors and has difficulty in picking up mistakes, hands you a letter with no typing errors, it is important to recognize that. The recognition needs to be immediate, so that it reinforces the new behaviour you want to encourage. However, recognition loses its value if it is too liberally used. Remember, the value of recognition is in reinforcing positive behaviour which is not normally characteristic of the individual and therefore motivates the individual to continue their positive behaviour. Having said that, however, there are also situations where recognizing consistently high performance is appropriate, so that the individual does not 'go off the boil'!

5. Communication

Communication is an interesting dimension of motivation, because it impacts more when it is absent than when it is present. In other words, effective communication is unlikely to be a great motivator; but the lack of it will be quite a strong demotivator. Think of communication here in its widest meaning: a two-way process whereby the views of others are sought and information is clearly given to others. Experience suggests that organizations undergoing large-scale change programmes often have to manage the side-effects of low morale. If you ask individuals what lies behind their demotivation, lack of communication is often cited as an important factor. They do not know the direction the company is going in, why certain decisions are being made, and they have very little say on the impact managerial decisions are having at their particular level.

6. Clear leadership

Although leadership has been given a chapter of its own, it is important in the context of motivation and will get a brief mention here. Providing individuals with a rationale and a business case for change is important for motivation. This point is raised by Tom Peters (1982), when he highlights the importance of competitive analysis as a motivational factor; in other words, until managers start informing others of what the competition is doing and how that is impacting on their own business, commitment and motivation to change will be half-hearted. There are also other barriers to motivation, such as unequal distribution of work, poor working conditions, etc. Clear leadership is a catalyst in ensuring that these barriers are removed. It is difficult to improve morale when debilitating factors have been left unaddressed over a long period of time.

7. Understanding individual expectations

All individuals are different and what motivates one person could 'switch-off' another. As a manager it is important to understand and recognize the varying aspirations and needs of employees. Managing expectations is an important feature of motivation. For example, most individuals perform much better when they enjoy what they do – if you can identify these areas and engineer opportunities for the individual which match their expectations, you are well on the road to getting the best from that individual. Motivation is determined by the level of desire and commitment to achieve certain objectives. By identifying what those desires are – for example to have more responsibility, to be more highly paid, to become a project manager – and then creating the means by which the individual can achieve these desires, you will have gone a long way to generating commitment to the goal. (Case History 12.2 has more on this.)

8. Being in the driving seat

There is a theme running through many of the points made above, which is based on the psychological concept of 'locus of control'. This concept is not just applicable to motivation, but for the purposes of this chapter we will look at it from a fairly narrow perspective. The concept suggests that an individual can either have an *external* or an *internal* locus of control. In the case of the former, an individual feels that external factors (ie, ones outside of their control) are important in determining how successful they will be in life and work. An individual with an internal locus of control, however, considers themselves as being in the driving seat, where they actively determine what happens in their personal and working lives. It is their own efforts which determine their success or otherwise. The interesting point though, and it is a generalization, is that those who feel less in control of their life and environment (external locus of control) are likely to be far less motivated than those who feel they control life. 'There is no point...'; 'What's the use...'; 'Nothing changes...' are phrases likely to be used by those who are demotivated, while 'Let's have a go...'; 'It's worth a try...'; 'I'm sure we can do it', are likely be heard from those who are motivated and who have an internal locus of control. As a manager you could change the belief that 'I am not in control', by empowering, by devolving responsibility and authority to those that work with you, and in so doing, create a more motivated workforce. Create an organization where individuals are geared to an internal locus of control and where they are in greater control of their environment. Case History 12.3 demonstrates how, even through redundancy, organizations can make individuals feel they are in control of their futures. By ensuring individuals are accountable and have the necessary skills and resources to deliver, you have taken a big step in ridding the organization of 'finger-pointing' and laying the blame at others' door.

THE KEY PRINCIPLES OF MOTIVATION

There are several prominent theories on the subject of motivation. While each is not complete in itself, they collectively provide a useful perspective.

Some of the earliest pieces of work shedding light on this subject were the Hawthorn studies (Mayo, 1975). These studies started off by looking at environmental factors effecting productivity, but the findings soon indicated that non-environmental factors were just as important, if not more so, in effecting productivity.

The studies, named after the Hawthorn works of the Western Electric company, took place during the 1920s and '30s. The studies were set up to see what relationship existed between productivity and various physical conditions such as temperature and lighting. Despite altering the conditions for control and experimental groups, they noticed that for both groups productivity remained high. After trying numerous permutations the researchers concluded that *psychological* rather than physical factors were influencing productivity. The researchers attributed the increase in productivity in both groups to the fact that they were being observed – the phenomenon of having researchers observe them in the work context was sufficient to improve productivity. The implication for motivation, therefore, is that *individuals perform better if they think someone is taking an interest in their work*.

Another important name in the field of motivation is Abraham Maslow (1971) and his theory on the hierarchy of needs (shown in Figure 12.2). Maslow put forward the case that motivation was linked to individuals' needs, and that there was a hierarchy from the most fundamental to the highest, which he called 'self-actualization'. There are five levels to his hierarchy:

Level 5: self-actualization for personal growth and fulfilment.

Level 4: esteem needs for power and recognition.

Level 3: social and affection needs for inclusion and warmth.

Level 2: safety needs for security and stability.

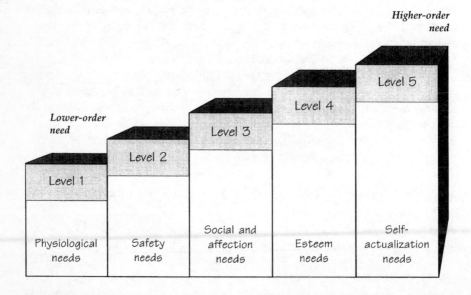

Figure 12.2 *Maslow's hierarchy of needs*

Level 1: physiological needs to survive, eat, sleep, etc.

According to Maslow, individuals work their way up the hierarchy, but each level of needs remains dependent on the levels below.

In the mid 1960s, another significant contribution was Herzberg's two-factor theory (1966). His work concentrated on the factors which caused job satisfaction and dissatisfaction. Using a technique called 'critical incident' (described in Case History 10.3) he asked individuals to recall incidents in their jobs that had given them strong feelings of either satisfaction or dissatisfaction. He then asked them to describe the causes in each case. Based on an analysis of their descriptions of what happened and why, Herzberg suggested a theory of what lay behind job satisfaction and dissatisfaction. Job satisfaction is the result of what Herzberg called *motivators*. These were factors such as having a sense of achievement, opportunities for personal development, and the sense of doing a task well. Dissatisfaction, on the other hand, was more likely to be attributed to *hygiene* factors. These included such things as money, the working environment and company policy. According to the theory, motivators and hygiene factors have different effects. If you want to remove dissatisfaction, improve the hygiene factors. However, improving them beyond a certain level (ie, removing the dissatisfaction) will not bring about an increase in satisfaction. The only way satisfaction will increase is by giving more of the motivators. The converse also applies, namely, providing more of the motivators will not by itself remove dissatisfaction.

Both Herzberg and Maslow are prominent names in the field of motivation. It is worth mentioning, however, that their theories are not always supported by experimental research; it appears that their theories hold up to investigation in certain situations but not in others. It is therefore useful to measure the *real impact* of your interventions on motivation if you are basing them on the work of Herzberg and Maslow.

Case History 12.1

Motivational Best Practice

It is important to appreciate how organizational issues have a strong bearing on the level of motivation experienced by individuals. The following is a compilation of best practices, noted by the author.

Clear vision and objectives

It is important that the organizations articulate the company vision – the goals it is striving to achieve – and translate it into what this means for the individual. The way successful organizations do this is by providing clear objectives, *not* restricting job descriptions. If you want a sign that individuals are not motivated, listen out for the number of times you hear: 'That is not my problem...; I'm not paid to do that...; it's more than my job's worth...' These signals demonstrate that the organization is not enabling and motivating individuals to maximize their contribution to the business.

Removing barriers

With the best will in the world, motivating employees is difficult if there are organizational barriers such as interdepartmental rivalry or conflict. Take the example of the service centre of a major bank, which processes cheques and direct debits for the branches. Branches used to see the service centre staff as inept, always sending information back late; while the service centre staff felt branch staff did not appreciate how difficult and laborious their role was. Motivation in the service centre was poor, because their main customer (the branches) did not value the nature of their work. In response to this, the bank adopted greater job rotation, so that branch staff experienced what service centre staff had to do and vice versa. This relatively simple act removed the major barrier to motivation: the feeling that other parts of the organization undervalued and did not appreciate the benefits they provided.

Rewarding equitably

Few things 'turn-off' employees more than a feeling of being unfairly rewarded. Effective remuneration strategies reward not just *what* individuals deliver but also *how* they do so. Competency-based reward strategies are becoming more widespread: alongside the actual objectives achieved, consideration is given to the extent an individual coached or developed others; or the extent to which they demonstrated customer-orientated behaviour. If an organization wants to create a motivated workforce it has to be consistent and fair in the way it rewards individuals. Nothing sends out a clearer message to employees than acknowledging and rewarding behaviour which embodies the ethos and values of what the organization is striving to achieve. More effective organizations also use a number of methods by which to reward, for example: providing opportunities for sabbaticals, which will enable individuals to learn and add value to the business; secondments to other parts of the business, which provide a challenge and an opportunity for growth. In other words, they try to match the needs of individuals with how they are rewarded.

Case History 12.2

Motivation – a Complex Formula of Expectations, Personality and Environment

This case history conveys the complex nature of motivation. The example is of a recruitment consultancy, but the lessons it provides are relevant to most organizations.

This is the story of Jones and Jones Executive Search and Selection (not the real name of the company). Its services centred on executive search and selection at the senior management level. Each consultant had to both sell their own work and carry it out, so there was a strong focus on self-sufficiency. The company encouraged consultants to think of themselves as running their own business, each having their own geographical area they were responsible for.

So what differentiated the more successful from less successful consultants? Levels of motivation was most certainly an important differentiator. The more effective consultants had a sense of purpose in their work and carried out the rather mundane tasks really well, eg 'cold-calling' and sending out regular mail-shots and following them up. One factor closely associated with motivation is personality. While all the consultants may have started of with a great deal of enthusiasm for 'cold-calling', very few sustained it. Resilience, tenacity and a positive outlook are important for sustained motivation. Whereas the less effective got 'switched-off' by rejections, the more effective stuck at it, rationalizing the rejections as part and parcel of the job and did not take them personally. Their positive outlook focused their minds on the fact that with each rejection the next call was far more likely to result in some interest and a sales visit. The more effective consultants also had a very clear idea of what they wanted from their jobs – to earn a lot of money! – and were motivated to that end. One could argue that it was purely this motivation of earning 'big bucks' which enabled consultants to rationalize the rejections, rather than personality itself.

Environment too is important in determining levels of motivation. The more effective consultants tended by and large to be quite insular, having no real need for contact with others; they preferred to come and go as they pleased, requiring little support from the company. These preferences nicely matched the culture of the company – use your own initiative to get results, resolve any issues off your own back and let's see what your results are at the monthly sales meetings. Those who 'hated' the job did so because of this 'mechanistic' and solitary existence. The environment was a key demotivating factor. Turnover for recruitment consultants was very high – an irony given that you would expect a recruitment company to get this one thing right at least.

An important reason why the culture and environment of the company was such a 'turn-off' was that consultants were joining with unrealistic and false expectations. In particular, young MBAs who had worked with big multinationals found it very difficult to come to terms working in this vastly different culture.

In short, personality, environment and expectations are inextricably linked to motivation. All three factors are required in equal portions for sustaining motivation.

Case history 12.3

Achieving the Near Impossible – Motivating Staff through Redundancy

The is the case of Finco, a life assurance company which collects premiums directly from customers' homes each month. Its issue was: how do we motivate employees to stay with us and achieve sales targets, after we have announced that within six months we will no longer be requiring their services? Finco had decided it was far more cost-effective to move their customers to direct debit, rather than employing administrators to go round collecting the premiums. Its IT systems, however, would not be ready for a further six months. The dilemma, therefore, was how to announce the redundancies amongst the administrators – with their jobs no longer being required – while at the same time avoiding them leaving and taking their customers with them. Finco decided to adopt the following strategy:

Come clean: inform the administrators that redundancies would be made, and present the business case behind that decision. Inform them also that for the remaining six months they were still required to meet their performance objectives.

Support: Finco could have employed an outplacement consultancy and 'washed' its hands of its responsibilities, taking comfort in the fact that it was doing everything it could to help the administrators get further employment. However, what Finco decided to do was implement a number of support packages. The first was to offer administrators training and development to be redeployed within Finco as financial consultants. The second was to offer training and some financial assistance to people to help them set up their own business, but as a supplier to Finco.

The thinking behind this was, why lose individuals to the competition, given the investment already made in training over the years?

Objectivity and fairness: Finco decided that it would not make administrators redundant arbitrarily, would use a more meaningful process, based on previous performance data and assessment centre data. The assessment centre would enable candidates to 'preview' key elements of the jobs they were applying for and allow assessors (the managers they would be reporting to) to make objective assessments.

By preventing damaging rumours through *decisive* communication and putting people in the picture with the options available to them, Finco was able to ensure that those that clearly wanted 'out' could do so, with a generous package; while those who wanted a future with the company were given every opportunity to demonstrate what they had to offer. Given the importance of this six-month transitionary period, maintaining motivation of employees was critical to the longer term success of Finco. The motivation of people who were to be made redundant was as important as those who were to stay, which made this such a sensitive issue for the company.

KEY ACTION AND LEARNING POINTS

1. What have been the main learning points for you in this chapter and how can you apply them?

2. What are the main motivational issues facing you and what plan of action do you need, in what timescales and with what resources?

3. Which individuals (colleagues and people who report to you) can you call on as 'motivation agents', ie individuals who can have an important impact in positively motivating others?

LEARNING POINTS FROM THE CASE HISTORIES

In the case of Finco, the main learning point is that organizations have an important role to play in ensuring that individuals remain motivated even under extreme situations. With so many other things on the go at the same time, it would be relatively easy for senior managers to overlook a factor such as motivation. Effective communication is often undervalued as a factor which can improve motivation, especially during times of change, where individuals are often desperate to find out what is happening and where they stand.

Successful organizations get into successful habits, which sustain levels of motivation. These include having a clear sense of where the company is going, what its short and longer term objectives are and how these impact on the individual. Successful organizations create an environment where individuals are allowed to fulfil their potential through knowing what is expected of them. Clarification of goals and objectives enables individuals to 'get on with it', not wasting time wondering if they are on the right track. Closely allied to this is removing barriers which frustrate and impede performance, even though these barriers may serve an administrative purpose. Finally, successful organisations create 'win-win' environments where effort and commitment on the individual's part are equitably rewarded by the organization.

In the case of Jones and Jones, the key point is that motivation is strongly person-centred: what motivates one individual is likely to 'turn-off' another. A matching of expectations and reality is important for motivation to exist. Equally, one's values and personal characteristics need to be congruent with the role. Don't expect an outgoing, gregarious, 'wheeler-dealer' to get a great deal of motivation from doing a job which is desk-bound and offers little interaction with others!

SUMMARY

The business case

A motivated workforce is a valuable business asset. Many of today's business trends are heavily reliant on a well-motivated workforce. In flatter organizational structures, with greater emphasis on self-managed teams and reliance on self-learning, motivation is a key component for success. If organizations are to succeed in major change programmes, the drive and impetus for them comes from a *desire* to succeed. Where large scale downsizing has taken place, it is important for those remaining to look to the future, not the past. Where new working practices need to be introduced in a short period of time, a 'can-do' attitude among employees is imperative if the business is not to suffer long-term set backs. The bottom line is that an intangible such as motivation can have an enormous tangible impact on the business – both positive and negative.

Putting it into practice

Organizational factors and the behaviours demonstrated by managers have an impact on motivation. There are some 'golden' rules which promote motivation. The first is involvement: where individuals feel they have a say in the way things happen in an organization, are consulted and are actively involved in the decision-making process. It is much easier to get excited by something which you have an involvement in than with something which is imposed on you. Responsibility is another important factor which is closely associated with motivation. Achieving challenging objectives outside of one's 'comfort zone' and having the responsibility to take decisions and be accountable is another important dimension of motivation. Knowing that what one does is valued and recognized by one's boss is also important and reason why delegating is so important. In delegating to subordinates, a manager is sending out a clear message: 'I think you are competent and capable of a lot more'. Note, however, that delegation entails providing subordinates with challenging objectives – not mundane, run-of-the-mill work. Finally, providing subordinates with clear leadership, regular communication and recognizing achievements, are further factors within a manager's control which can directly influence levels of motivation.

The key principles

The prominent work on motivation are Herzberg's two-factor theory and Maslow's hierarchy of needs. Both theories contend that motivation is less reliant on tangible factors, such as money and working conditions, than on intangible factors, such as enjoying what one does, and gaining job satisfaction. Motivation and demotivation, therefore, are strongly person-centred. In other words, motivation is closely associated with psychological factors, and, as such, it would be relatively easy to 'switch-off' a high-performing individual by not praising them, or not acknowledging the contribution they are making to the business. The extent to which individuals need recognition will also be related to their psychological maturity. Self-confident, 'been there, seen it, done it' types will require less recognition than those who are less sure. Equally, those who have been through a difficult learning process will require constructive feedback and feel they have learnt from it.

References

Adair, John (1986) *Effective Teambuilding*, Gower, Aldershot.

Argyris, C (1991) Teaching smart people how to learn, *Harvard Business Review*, May–June.

Belasco, JA (1990) *Teaching the Elephant to Dance*, Hutchinson, London.

Belbin, Meredith (1981) *Management Teams: Why They Succeed or Fail*, Heinemann, London.

Bennis, W and Nanus, B (1985) *Leaders*, Harper and Row, London.

Berne, Eric (1972) *What Do You Say After You Say Hello?* Corgi, London.

Blake, RR and Mouton, JS (1964) *The Managerial Grid*, Gulf Publishing, Houston.

de Bono, Edward (1993) *Sur/petition: Going Beyond Competition*, HarperCollins, London.

Haeckel, H and Nolan, RL (1993) Managing by wire, *Harvard Business Review*, Sept–Oct.

Hamel, Gary and Prahalad, CK (1990) The core competence of the corporation, *Harvard Business Review*.

Hersey, P and Blanchard, KM (1982) *Management of Organizational Behaviour: Utilizing Human Resources*, Prentice-Hall, Englewood Cliffs, NJ.

Herzberg, F (1966) *Work and the Nature of Man*, World Publishing Cleveland, Ohio.

Jackson, Bryan (1993) Cited in Mike Thatcher's article; Toyota team system aims for 'mutual trust and respect', *Personnel Management Plus*, 4, 1.

Kaplan, R and Norton, D (1992) The balanced scorecard – measures that drive performance, *Harvard Business Review*, Jan–Feb.

Kolb, DA, Rubin IM and McIntyre, JM (1974) *Organisational Psychology: An Experiential Approach*, Prentice-Hall, Englewood Cliffs, NJ.

Maslow, AH (1971) *The Further Reaches of Human Nature*, Viking, New York.

Mayo, E (1975) *The Social Problems of an Industrial Civilization*, Routledge and Kegan Paul, London.

Nayak, P and Ketteringham, John M (1993) *Breakthroughs*, Mercury Business Books, Didcot, Oxon.

Normann, R and Ramirez, R (1993) From value chain to value constellation, *Harvard Business Review*, July–August.

O'Driscoll, T (1993), quoted in King Taylor, L, *Quality: Sustaining Customer Service*, Century, London.

Peters, Tom (1988) *Thriving on Chaos*, Macmillan, London.

Peters, T and Austin, N (1985) *A Passion for Excellence*, Fontana/Collins, London.

Porter, Michael (1965) *Competitive Advantage*, Free Press, New York.

Schein, Edgar (1993) How can organizations learn faster? The challenge of entering the Green Room, *Sloan Management Review*, winter.

Stalk, George, Evans, Philip and Shulman, Lawrence (1992) Competing on capabilities: the new rules of corporate strategy, *Harvard Business Review*, March–April.

Waitley, D (1994) *The New Dynamics of Winning*, Nicholas Brealey, London.

Whetten, C and Cameron, K (1991) *Developing Management Skills*, HarperCollins, London.

Womack, JP and Jones, DT (1994) From lean production to the lean enterprise, *Harvard Business Review*, March–April.

Index

Reader
Questionnaire

This combined book and software package is a new development. We would, therefore, welcome your feedback on the following:

1. Which aspects of the combined package did you find most useful?

    ....

    ....

2. Which aspects did you find least useful?

    ....

    ....

3. What other topics would be of interest to you in terms of interactive packages?

    e.g.: Managing change   ❑   Sales effectiveness   ❑

    Performance management   ❑   Other (please stipulate)   ❑

    Project management   ❑   ....

    ....

4. What other types of information/options might you expect from any future book/software package?

    ....

    ....

    ....

5. Do you require additional information about future publications/articles on self-development etc?   YES ❑   NO ❑

Your name ....   Home address ....

Company name ....   Address ....

Your position ....

Thank you for your help. Please return this questionnaire to: Dr Sukhwant Bal
c/o Kogan Page Ltd
120 Pentonville Rd
London N1 9JN

Loading the Software

TECHNICAL SPECIFICATIONS

We would recommend the following to help you to get the most from the software:

- 486SX 25 computer
- with Super VGA screen
- 1mb of RAM video card
- 4mb RAM
- Windows 3.1
- DOS 6.2

TO LOAD THE SOFTWARE

- Run Windows application
- open Programme Manager
- select File
- select Run
- in command line type a:setup
- follow screen instructions (ensure all files loaded onto default c:\comp)
- once installation is complete, double-click on Interactive Manager icon to run the programme. See introduction section for further information on how to use the software.